EPHESIANS...
LIVING WITH THE ARMOR INTACT!

By
Sonie Curtis

Cover Art by Nancy James

Bible Study Workbook using the
Guided Discovery Study System™

Ephesians
Living with the Armor Intact!
Bible Study Workbook

ISBN: 978-996467803

Printed in the United States of America
Copyright © 2015 – TrueJoy Publications, L.L.C.

TrueJoy Publications, L.L.C.
P.O. Box 311
Rockford, MI 49341-1011

All rights reserved. This book is protected by the copyright laws of the United States of America. No part of this book may be reproduced or transmitted in any form or by any means, electronic or mechanical, including photocopying, recording or by any information storage and retrieval system, without permission in writing from the publisher.

Unless otherwise noted, Scripture quotations are taken from the Holy Bible, *King James Version,* public domain.

For additional copies or questions contact:
TrueJoy Publications, L.L.C., P.O. Box 311, Rockford, MI 49341-1011.
or
truejoypublications@gmail.com

DEDICATION

There are so many people to thank for their love, support, time and effort which they have put into helping complete this work. Thank you to all of my friends, family, and those who have attended my Bible studies.

To the bible study ladies who have been so faithful to attend class, do their homework, give me their honest input, challenging me to delve deeper into the Word for the truth that is contained in it. Also, for their continued supportive loving kindness as we serve the Lord together. I cherish the relationships that have developed through the years of sharing the Word and our lives together. I will never be the same from the impact each one of you has had on my life.

To all those who personally worked on this project from editing, testing the book for individual study, graphic design, artistic talent, taking my picture, helping with cover design, teaching me programs on the computer, rewording, suggestions for clarity and things I can't even think of right now. You are all amazing people that God has put in my life. I am so blessed to know you all!!

Thank you to my family for all your love and support and always being willing to help out. I have the best family in the world!!

ENDORSEMENTS

"This study in Ephesians is rich with revelation. The lessons don't allow you to gloss over any text, but cause you to see the importance of each word written by Paul. It is a 'must study' for any Believer who hungers for more of God." Susan Foster

"Ephesians. Word by word. Verse by verse. This is an enlightening study that will bring the student to a new level of understanding of Paul's love and care for the church at Ephesus. The value of knowing who we are in Christ is paramount to our every day living. Sonie emphasizes that in each lesson. Take the armor of God...put it on...and don't take it off. This may be a new thought, but valuable to our Christianity as we walk in the hope that Christ has for us." Marlene Gardner

"Sonie's Bible studies take you into the center of God's heart. One can't help but see God's truth as Sonie shines a light on His Word . Thought provoking, enlightening, challenging and forever life changing. Jump into a Bible study by Sonie and you will discover who you are and why you were put on planet earth." Sandra Warren

"I so appreciate how this Bible study gets us into the Word of God for ourselves, to discover what it really says, instead of relying on preconceived notions or someone else's commentary." Stephanie Sousa

"Dissecting each verse within a book brings greater understanding of the Word and how to apply it to our everyday life." Nancy James

"In this study, Sonie gives great in-depth teaching covering Ephesians. It is encouraging and enlightening for any believer. Wonderful for a group or individual study!" Beth Clayton

"Learning about Ephesians through this method of study has opened my eyes and heart with the understanding of who we are and what we are given. It has helped me to grow spiritually. Ephesians is a must study!" Betsy Smith

"Sonie's Bible study emphasizes the "love of God," that I had not grasped beforehand. I am experiencing much freedom in the simplicity of God's grace. I have a better understanding now of what Jesus accomplished through His death, burial and resurrection." Jan Rau

INTRODUCTION

Have you ever heard the song titled "Limitless" by Planetshakers? While meditating on the concept of God being limitless, I wondered, "If God is limitless then why does he seem limited in the lives of so many Believers?" The only factor I could come up with was **us**. We limit Him! And we don't even realize it! If every Believer could really get a handle on what God has provided through Christ, we would never be the same. The church would be what God had intended us to be from the beginning, sharing in the very life of Christ from glory to glory. (2 Cor. 3:18)

I am so excited for you as you journey through the book of Ephesians with this study. The Bible is the most life changing book in the world. There are treasures of wisdom in the Bible awaiting us to understand and apply to our lives. The Word shows us how to live complete fulfilled lives with Jesus at the center.

Paul told Timothy that the inspired Word of God has the power to make us wise and completely equipped for good works (2 Timothy 3:15-17). These good works are His workmanship in us to bring us to that place of "Christ in you, the hope of glory." (Eph. 2:10; Col 1:27) This being the hearts desire of every Believer, I trust this study will help you on your journey.

Ephesians contains the most comprehensive revelation of the Believers union in the finished work of Christ than any other book of the Bible. The book of Ephesians can be grouped into two divisions of content. Chapters **1-3** deal with **who we are** and **what we have** in Christ because of God's grace. Chapters **4-6** deal with **living daily in this knowledge** of who we are and what we have because of the completed work of Christ.

I believe that Paul's intent in writing Ephesians was to show the place and position that believers presently have available "In Christ" (as He is seated on the throne) that is far above any circumstance that could be encountered on earth. Furthermore, this position not only applies to the individual, but to a complete body of Believers, working as one In Christ (one mind and one body).

My prayer as you go through this study is for you to personally experience what Paul was writing to the Ephesians. To know, without a doubt, who you are "In Christ" and let the Word *change your life*!

Prayerfully together with you on this joyful journey,
Sonie

TABLE OF CONTENTS

DEDICATION 3
ACKNOWLEDGEMENTS 4
INTRODUCTION. 6
HOW AND WHY TO USE THIS STUDY 9
ANSWER KEY – How to use 11
READING LOG – How to use 12

LEADER SECTION
    Leader Guide 14
    Helpful Tips for Leaders 16
    Ice Breaker 17
    Getting to Know You 19

HISTORY SECTION
    Ephesians History 22

WORKSHEET SECTION
    Scripture Worksheet 1 26
    Worksheet 1 27
    Scripture Worksheet 2 34
    Worksheet 2 35
    Scripture Worksheet 3 44
    Worksheet 3 45
    Summary Chapters 1-3 51
    Scripture Worksheet 4 54
    Worksheet 4 55
    Scripture Worksheet 5 62
    Worksheet 5 63
    Scripture Worksheet 6 70
    Worksheet 6 71
    Scripture Worksheet 7 78
    Worksheet 7 79
    Scripture Worksheet 8 88
    Worksheet 8 89
    Scripture Worksheet 9 98
    Worksheet 9 99

Table of Contents continued ...

SPIRITUAL WARFARE WORKSHEET SECTION
Introduction to Spiritual Warfare – The Armor 107
    Scripture Spiritual Warfare Worksheet 1 108
    Spiritual Warfare Worksheet 1 109
    Recap Worksheet 1 114
    Scripture Spiritual Warfare Worksheet 2 116
    Spiritual Warfare Worksheet 2 117
    Recap Worksheet 2 124
    Scripture Spiritual Warfare Worksheet 3 126
    Spiritual Warfare Worksheet 3 127
    Recap Worksheet 3 135
    Scripture Spiritual Warfare Worksheet 4 136
    Spiritual Warfare Worksheet 4 137

ANSWER KEY SECTION
    Worksheet 1 147
    Worksheet 2 153
    Worksheet 3 161
    Worksheet 4 167
    Worksheet 5 173
    Worksheet 6 179
    Worksheet 7 187
    Worksheet 8 195
    Worksheet 9 203

SPIRITUAL WARFARE ANSWER KEY SECTION
    Spiritual Warfare Worksheet 1 211
    Recap Worksheet 1 216
    Spiritual Warfare Worksheet 2 217
    Recap Worksheet 2 224
    Spiritual Warfare Worksheet 3 225
    Recap Worksheet 3 232
    Spiritual Warfare Worksheet 4 233

KNOWING JESUS 241

REMEMBERING THE WORD – MEMORIZATION 96

HOW AND WHY TO USE THIS STUDY

If you're like me and have to make an effort to carve out a few moments to spend in the Word, then you want to make the most of that time and get something out of it. It's frustrating to come away with limited understanding of seemingly mysterious passages.

Have you ever run across a verse that seems to divert from the subject of the surrounding verses. Or how about, reading along, getting a pretty good understanding about what the writer is talking about, when out of nowhere there is a verse that just doesn't make sense? I call these *"skip over verses."* Not having the time to do a deep study to find out why this verse was even in this portion of scripture, I *skip over it*.

Since then, I have developed a study system that I call the **Guided Discovery Study System™** that can, in less time than a theological college course, help to answer questions like "Why is this verse here?" and "What is the author really trying to say?" I believe that scripture that seems out of place is there for a reason and I'm just not asking the right questions to get the right meaning.

Another reason I developed the **Guided Discovery Study System™** is the value of self-discovery. We tend to remember, on a deeper heart level, those things that we discover on our own! It seems easy for me to let someone tell me what the Bible says, but unless I purpose to take it to heart and do something with it, it is only words forgotten in very little time. When I discover Bible truth and really think about the effect that it has on me, it will be placed in my heart for later reference and put to use.

The goal of the **Guided Discovery Study System™** is to bring clarity by asking questions that guide the participant to discover the contents and meanings contained in the scriptures while keeping that information in the **context** of the letter or book of the bible.

The format addresses these context questions:
1. **Who** is talking and to whom are they writing?
2. **What** is the subject and what is the goal of the writer for his readers regarding that subject?
3. **Where** did the events take place or where will they take place?
4. **When** was the time frame for the events or subject?
5. **How** does this apply to my life?

The following are the components that make up the **Guided Discovery Study System™**.

- **History** – The history is included at the beginning of the WORKSHEET SECTION and should be the first place that you start. Understanding the history and culture at the time of the writing of Ephesians also plays an integral part in our experiencing, in our own lives, what is contained in the scripture.
- **King James Version (KJV)** – All of the questions for this study have been taken from The King James Version of the bible, unless otherwise noted. The questions are geared to help you break down the scripture to gain the maximum understanding. Therefore, it is beneficial to use the King James version for the sake of congruency. However, sometimes other versions will give clarity to what is being studied. At times you will be asked to use another version of the bible. This is notated by **AOV** indicating **Any Other Version**.
- **Weekly Worksheets** – The worksheets are set-up with numbers corresponding to the chapter and verse being studied. The worksheets will guide you through the scriptures as you answer questions relating to what you are reading in the Word. The worksheets can be broken into daily studies by completing two pages of a worksheet per day or they can be completed throughout the week as your time allows. The worksheets are laid out in a verse-by-verse format. Additional reference verses will clarify certain portions of scripture being studied.
- **Person opinion questions** - Occasionally you will be asked for your opinion regarding certain topics. Do your best to answer these questions as they will help in understanding scripture or clarify truths of which you are not aware.
- **Commentaries** – Commentaries are not recommended for this type of study. This really is about God speaking to you, showing you the truth of the scriptures. It is best to get your answers directly from the scripture.
- **Reading Log** – At the top of each worksheet you will be asked to read a portion of scripture daily. This scripture corresponds to the worksheet being studied. A READING LOG is included to track your daily reading. See the READING LOG section for more information.
- **Answer Keys** – ANSWER KEYS are provided in the back of the book. Use the ANSWER KEYS after you have completed an entire worksheet section only to check your answers and obtain additional information regarding the scripture section being studied. See the ANSWER KEYS section for a more detailed description.
- **Group study** – To complete this as a group study, refer to the LEADERS GUIDE.

Prayerfully begin this study thanking the Holy Spirit as He teaches and guides you into all truth. ENJOY!

ANSWER KEY GUIDE

ANSWER KEYS are provided for all the worksheets in this study.

ANSWER KEYS contain the following:
- Answers to every question taken from the scripture or other sources that are referenced.
- Greek or Hebrew meanings of words.
- References to verses that need further explanation.
- More in-depth answers with references from similar or related scriptures.

To obtain the most benefit from this type of study, the ANSWER KEY should be used to check your answers <u>after</u> the worksheets have been completed through individual study. For group study the ANSWER KEY will be used by the leader.

The ultimate purpose of this study is for the participant to see for themselves what is contained in the scriptures being examined. Often times we read and understand a verse based on how someone else has explained it to us in the past, or based on wrong assumptions. The **Guided Discovery Study System™** will help you discover for yourself the contents of scripture which may be different from first impressions or past instruction. This study system carefully considers context of the author's culture and original language and also compares scripture with scripture.

LEADERS: See the leader guide for instructions on using the ANSWER KEY within a group setting.

READING LOG

For a deeper depth of study of the book of Ephesians I have included a reading log below. The object of the reading log is to keep track of your daily reading as you study the book of Ephesians. In order to get the most from the scripture being studied we need to keep it before our eyes **daily**. By reading the scripture portion everyday you will gain a better understanding of the scripture. Simply circle the day after you read that days portion of scripture.

Daily reading stirs our memory. We know that to achieve advancement in anything it takes doing that thing over and over again. As we saturate ourselves with the book of Ephesians we will become aware of scriptures that we might not have really given great thought to otherwise. Daily reading also helps us to remember where certain scriptures are located in the book of Ephesians.

In your daily reading time, ask God to show you what he wants you to see today that will impact your life or the lives of those you influence. We are so blessed to have access to the very words of God. The words that God spoke thousands of years ago have the same power resident in them as when God spoke them. Let them do the job God sent them to do, work to change lives.

EPHESIANS READING LOG

Worksheet 1 1:1-16
Day 1 2 3 4 5 6 7

Worksheet 2 1:17-2:5
Day 1 2 3 4 5 6 7

Worksheet 3 2:6-22
Day 1 2 3 4 5 6 7

Worksheet 4 3:1-15
Day 1 2 3 4 5 6 7

Worksheet 5 3:16-4:10
Day 1 2 3 4 5 6 7

Worksheet 6 4:11-27
Day 1 2 3 4 5 6 7

Worksheet 7 4:28-5:14
Day 1 2 3 4 5 6 7

Worksheet 8 5:15-27
Day 1 2 3 4 5 6 7

Worksheet 9 5:29-6:9
Day 1 2 3 4 5 6 7

Worksheets 10-13 contain additional scriptures from other books of the bible. There will be no daily reading for those worksheets.

LEADERS SECTION

LEADER GUIDE

My goal for this study is to keep the focus on connecting and empowering Believer's to rise above circumstances and allow the Holy Spirit to show them how to make the truth of the bible relevant in their daily lives.

Below is a suggested format for leading weekly groups using the **Guided Discovery Study System™**.

<u>Week 1</u> As a leader, the goal for your first meeting is to get to know each other and teach others how to use the study guide by going through it section by section. In addition, you will complete part of the first worksheet together and assign the remainder of the first worksheet as homework.

- PRAY: Open the meeting with prayer.
- ICE BREAKER: Begin your studies with something fun to help everyone feel comfortable with each other. I have included one ice breaker in this section that you can use or find one online that suits your group. I have each table fill them in and I read them aloud after they are completed. This activity can also be done with a smaller group. This should be limited to 15 minutes.
- WORKBOOK SECTIONS: Together read the Introduction, How to use this study, and the description page from each section of the workbook. (Worksheets, Answer Keys, The Armor) This will help familiarize everyone with the workbook.
- GETTING ACQUAINTED: There is a GETTING AQUAINTED sheet included in each workbook that can be completed and torn out of the workbook for your use. This sheet allows you to have a more personal connection with the members of your group and gives you an idea of how to pray for them for the duration of your study.
- HISTORY: Go over the History portion of the study. The history and the culture at the time of the writing plays an important part in understanding the scripture and its content. Having a clear picture of what the readers of Paul's original letters were encountering in their own lives will better equip us in applying the appropriate truths to ours.
- WORKSHEETS: Do the first page of WORKSHEET ONE together as a group. This will familiarize the group with the format of the worksheets.
- ANSWER KEYS: ANSWER KEYS have been provided. Many Greek and Hebrew word meanings are contained in this section. Although it may seem tedious at first to refer to the ANSWER KEY for the word meanings it is essential to understanding the truth of what the author is really saying (God saying through the author). Help group members develop an enthusiasm for these discoveries. If you act like it is exciting (or boring),

others will think so also. Refer to the ANSWER KEY GUIDE for a detailed description, reason and use of the ANSWER KEYS.
- HOMEWORK: In preparation for the next meeting, instruct group members to complete the remainder of WORKSHEET ONE to be ready for discussion. Encourage your members <u>not</u> to 'cheat' and use the Answer Key. They can get the most benefit from the class if they discover answers for themselves. Answers will be revealed at the next meeting.

**LEADERS ONLY: After you have completed your worksheet, compare it with the answer key to be aware of any additional information such as, Greek meanings of words, or other related material to be ready for the following weeks meeting.

<u>Week 2-14</u> As the leader, you will facilitate group discussion asking members to share answers to the WORKSHEET questions they have prepared as homework. Also you will lead the group through the ANSWER KEYS. This allows the group members to check their answers and think through the truth during class.

- Read or have someone read the portion of scripture being studied for that week from the worksheet.
- Ask each question individually and let the members give their answers. If you hear a 'wrong answer' simply ask others what they got for that one. **Very Important:** Some answers may differ. That's okay, but you do want truth to be revealed. So, occasionally refer together to the ANSWER KEY. Previous teaching, wrong assumption or past understanding has taught us differently. The purpose of this type of study is so that we can see now what is really contained in the scripture and let the Holy Spirit continue to teach us.
- Ask them to be more descriptive in their answers. For example: If salvation is the answer to a question, how would they describe what salvation is to them or if they were explaining it to someone else. Sometimes (christian-ese) words become so common for believers that we don't realize that we have lost the true meaning of the word. You can refer to the ANSWER KEY for descriptions regarding these types of words.
- Assign the next worksheet as homework for the next meeting.

HELPFUL TIPS FOR LEADERS:

- Try to have NAME TAGS available for each week. This will help you and the other members get and stay connected.

- Complete YOUR WORKSHEET for each week prior to referring to the ANSWER KEY. This will help you in understanding what the other members are going through if any questions should arise. Refer to the ANSWER KEY to check your answers prior to attending the next class. (I know that I have said this several times, but it is so important in helping us retain information if we experience the learning process for ourselves without depending on someone else to do the thinking for us.)

- One complication in doing a study directly from the Word is that some past misunderstandings or interpretations of scripture may cause **conflicting answers among group members.** Here is how I address these conflicts. I ask everyone to look at the verse as if we are reading it for the first time to really grasp what the verse is saying. Then refer to the Answer Key containing word meanings and any other related information. **One place in this study where this situation arose was at Ephesians 4:26. Based on prior teachings, some members have thought that this verse means that you can be angry as long as you forgive before you go to bed. By looking at the Greek and comparing verse 26 with verse 30 and with Jesus' teaching on the subject, this could be saying something else. A more descriptive explanation will be given during the study of this section. We should always let scripture explain scripture. We shouldn't guess at things just because it sounds good to us.

Most of all: **Have FUN!!** Enjoy one another as you learn together.

ICE BREAKER

Leaders:
- One sheet per table.
- Fill in blanks below with names or numbers for each question from the people at each table.
- After complete, read aloud to compare answers from each table.

Who has the most number of children? _____ # of children _____
Who has the least number of children? _____ # of children _____
Who lives the furthest away? _____
Who has the most grand-children? _____
How many have or had a physical labor job? _____
How many have or had a sit down job? _____
Total number of college degrees? _____
Who has the oldest child? _____ Age _____
Who has the youngest child? _____ Age _____
How many live in the same state where they were born? _____
How many went out of state for a vacation? _____
Who has lived outside the U.S.? _____ Where? _____
Who has moved the most? _____ # times _____
How many play an instrument? _____
How many have family that live out of state? _____
How many drive a mini-van? _____
How many know who Dick Van Dyke is? _____
How many have gone camping for vacations ? _____
How many have a Pinterest account? _____
How many like to do crafts? _____
How many have never done a Bible Study before? _____

If you are excited to be here all of you yell out "Hallelujah".

GETTING TO KNOW YOU

Name:
Address:
Phone:

Circle one: Single   Married   Divorced   Widowed

Name of spouse:

Children: Name and Age

Hobbies:

Why are you taking this study and what do you hope to get out of it?

What can I be in agreement with you in prayer for the duration of this study?

HISTORY SECTION

EPHESIANS HISTORY

In order for us to get a clearer understanding of the letter Paul wrote to the Ephesians we need to understand what the Believers in Ephesus were experiencing at the time of Paul's writing. Let's look at a very small overview of the city of Ephesus to give us an idea of what was going on at the time.

History of the City of Ephesus
Ephesus was a main commercial center of Asia Minor. It was a leading seaport of its day located at the mouth of the Cayster River, making Ephesus a city extensive in its commercial trade. It was also known for its draw to idolatry with many temples to different gods. The dominate temple being the Temple of Artemis, a Greek goddess of fertility, also known as the Temple of Diana. The Temple of Artemis was three times the size as the Greek Parthenon and was known as one of the seven wonders of the world. It brought worshipers of Diana from all over the world causing the city to be buzzing with activity and commercial tourism.

Ephesus was also the intellectual meeting place where scholars and philosophers from around the world would come to share their knowledge in the Theater of Ephesus. This theater was one of the largest known in ancient times. It was a semicircular structure that could seat over 21,000 people.

Ephesus also contained the library of Celsus which was the largest of the ancient world with the most beautiful architecture of its day. Ephesus was estimated, by some scholars, to have a population of over 200,000 people. Second only in importance to Rome. It was in this Greek culture that Paul was able to build a church of possibly as many as 100,000 Christians of which Timothy was the first bishop.

It is also believed that John lived in Ephesus towards the end of his life. Rick Renner, in his extensive research for the book "A Light in the Darkness" said that John lived above the temple of Diana. John was constantly in the atmosphere of the worship practices and smells of incense being burned to the gods and yet he stood strong in the Lord throughout his life. John is a good example of not letting circumstances come before your relationship with God.

It is good for us to consider the culture in which the Ephesians were constantly being influenced as we study Paul's letter. There are issues that arise from their sphere of influence that we would not even consider as needing to be addressed in our lives. Although we can learn for the entirety of the Word of God, we must read it taking into consideration what the people of that day were experiencing.

Paul's connection to Ephesus
Acts 18:19–19:41 describes Paul's encounters with Ephesus. Paul ministered in Ephesus on his second and third missionary journeys. On his third missionary journey he spent about three years in Ephesus. He caused a problem with the idol makers sales because many of the Ephesians were becoming Christians and not worshiping gods or purchasing idols. The city was in an uproar with the thought that Diana would no longer be worshiped and the idol makers would loose their business. Paul's preaching of the Gospel caused the entire city to be in confusion. Therefore, the Christians in Ephesus encouraged Paul to leave and go to Macedonia.

Oh, that we Christians would cause such a stir that an entire city would be in confusion. How awesome would that be!!

Ephesians Content Overview

Ephesians can be broken into two distinct parts:
1. Chapters 1-3 deal with the Believers union with Christ.
   - Our position and calling in Christ.
   - The benefits of salvation by grace through faith.
   - The glorious things that are ours in Christ.
   - Contains two prayers asking God to grant the readers wisdom to be able to grasp the depth of the mysteries of Christ in you that Paul is revealing to them in Chapters 1-3.

2. Chapters 4-6 tell the practical aspects of walking out this union with Christ.
   - Conduct in relation to fellow believers.
   - Conduct in relation to unbelievers around them.
   - The relationship and conduct toward the Holy Spirit.
   - Conduct in relation to home and family.
   - Conduct and relationship to the devil.

History sources:
http://www.israeljerusalem.com/temple-of-diana-ephesus.htm
http://www.unmuseum.org/ephesus.htm

NOTES

WORKSHEET SECTION

SCRIPTURE - WORKSHEET 1
Ephesians 1:1-16

1 Paul, an apostle of Jesus Christ by the will of God, to the saints which are at Ephesus, and to the faithful in Christ Jesus:

2 grace *be* to you, and peace, from God our Father, and *from* the Lord Jesus Christ.

3 Blessed *be* the God and Father of our Lord Jesus Christ, who hath blessed us with all spiritual blessings in heavenly *places* in Christ:

4 according as he hath chosen us in him before the foundation of the world, that we should be holy and without blame before him in love:

5 having predestinated us unto the adoption of children by Jesus Christ to himself, according to the good pleasure of his will,

6 to the praise of the glory of his grace, wherein he hath made us accepted in the beloved.

7 in whom we have redemption through his blood, the forgiveness of sins, according to the riches of his grace;

8 wherein he hath abounded toward us in all wisdom and prudence;

9 having made known unto us the mystery of his will, according to his good pleasure which he hath purposed in himself:

10 that in the dispensation of the fulness of times he might gather together in one all things in Christ, both which are in heaven, and which are on earth; *even* in him:

11 in whom also we have obtained an inheritance, being predestinated according to the purpose of him who worketh all things after the counsel of his own will:

12 that we should be to the praise of his glory, who first trusted in Christ.

13 in whom ye also *trusted*, after that ye heard the word of truth, the gospel of your salvation: in whom also after that ye believed, ye were sealed with that Holy Spirit of promise,

14 which is the earnest of our inheritance until the redemption of the purchased possession, unto the praise of his glory.

15 Wherefore I also, after I heard of your faith in the Lord Jesus, and love unto all the saints,

16 cease not to give thanks for you, making mention of you in my prayers;

Worksheet 1
Ephesians 1:1 – 1:16

Read Ephesians 1:1-16 daily and prior to completing this worksheet.

V1 Who is the author of this letter?

What does Paul call himself in this letter?

How was Paul given this position?

To what two groups is this letter written?
1.
2.

V2 What two things does Paul want the Ephesians to have?
1.
2.

From where do these two things come?
1.
2.

2 Peter 1:2 How does Peter say that grace and peace can be increased in our lives?

Back to Ephesians 1:3 Who are the first two people who are blessed?
1.
2.

Who is the "us" that receives blessings from these two people?

Look up the word "blessed" in any source and give its meaning below:

What is the blessing that the "us" receives?

From where are they?

In whom are they?

If they are in Christ, try to name every place that Christ is, at this very moment?

In your opinion, what would you think spiritual blessings would be?

> DIGGING DEEPER: <u>Bless</u> is used in two ways.
>
> Hath blessed – Verb – It is the Greek word *eulogeō* which means "to cause to prosper, to make happy, to bestow blessings on." The phrase "who hath blessed us" is in the Greek aorist tense which means in the past there was a point in time that these blessings were acquired and given to believers. Paul is relating to believers what is already theirs in Christ. We should not be trying to obtain blessings from God but discovering and enjoying what we already have. Believers are heading from a victory that has already been won by Jesus Christ on our behalf.
>
> Spiritual blessings – Noun – It is the Greek word *eulogia* which means "a (concrete) blessing or benefit."
>
> Both of these forms of the word "bless" come from the root words *eu* and *logos*. *Eu* meaning "to be well off, prosper, or acting well." *Logos* refers to speaking or speech and is commonly referred to as "the sayings of God."
>
> When combined together they show us that these blessings come from and are received as we take the victorious Word and live it as the actions of our lives. That's exciting!!!

V4 Name who the following people are that are spoken about in this verse?

He _____

Him _____ (only the 1st one mentioned)

What did "he" do?

When did that last answer take place?

Who is the "we" in this verse? (V1 will help answer this)

What two things are listed as what we have been chosen to be?
1.   2.

V5 Look up the word "predestine" in any source?

To what does this verse say we have been predestined?

Through whom did this happen?

Why did this happen?

Explain what you think "to the good pleasure of his will" means?

What is the reason God choose to adopt us as his children through Jesus?

> DIGGING DEEPER: Predestine is the Greek word *proorizo* which conveys the meaning of being "appointed beforehand to obtain a thing." This same word is used in Romans 8:29 where Paul is describing to what believers have been predestined. "For whom he did foreknow, he also did predestinate *to be conformed to the image of his Son.*" Paul is addressing what God has done for believers. We have been predestined or appointed beforehand to be conformed to the image of Jesus. The word image conveys more than a similarity but a likeness that represents and manifests Jesus. Verse 4 says that we were "chosen in him" which means we are only predestined because we are in Christ. Christ was the chosen one and we are only chosen by God because we have chosen, by our decision, to be in Christ.

V6 Write out verse 6 from AOV of the bible:

_____
_____
_____

According to verses 5 and 6, what two reasons are given for God to adopt us as children?
- Because he was in a good mood that day.
- Because of his goodwill and plan.
- Because Jesus had nothing to do.
- To bring honor/praise to his glorious grace.

According to V6, what did God do that enabled us to be included in the beloved?

What was this adoption? As servants, As slaves, As friends, As children.

V7 How were we redeemed?

What comes to us because of this redemption?

Complete the following from verse 7: "We receive forgiveness for our failures/sins because of":

In your own words, explain what "grace" is?

> DIGGING DEEPER: Grace is the Greek word *charis*. Charis describes the loving kindness and favor of God that he bestows upon those who trust in him. Grace is salvation to man. It is God's power and ability that believers use to walk in God's ways, be strengthened in faith and obtain from God. It is the all-encompassing love of God.

V8 What verb(s) is used to describe how God gave us this grace?
KJV _____ AOV _____

How was this done? Circle all that apply:
"with judgment, evil, wisdom, suffering, good works, understanding."

Do you <u>feel</u> like you abound with wisdom and understanding?   Yes or No

Do you still have wisdom and understanding? Yes or No

How do you know that you have wisdom and understanding?

V9 What has been made known unto us?
KJV _____ AOV _____

This was made known according to what?

Complete the following from the verses below:
God's goodwill and plan or the good pleasure of his will was to do what 2 things?
V5
V9

This mystery was intended to be accomplished through whom?

V10 What time frame is this verse talking about?
KJV _____
AOV _____

What will happen?

All things will be gathered together from what two places?
1.   2.

In whom will these things be gathered together?

30

V11 What else has been obtained?

Through whom?

By what were we predestinated?

Complete the following according to this verse:
"God accomplishes everything…….."
    According to what's going on in the world.
    According to how we feel.
    According to what mankind says.
    According to his own design and will.

V12 Fill in the blanks from the KJV: "That _____ should be to the _____ of _____ _____ who first _____ in _____."

Look up the following words in any source and give their meaning:
Praise:
Glory:

What were those who first put their hope in Christ made to be?

In your opinion, describe what is "God's glory"?

In your own life, how do you think you bring praise to God's glory?

V13 In whom did the Ephesians trust? (V12 will help)

What did they have to hear before they trusted in Christ?

The KJV describes what they heard as what?

From your own life, how would you explain to someone what the "gospel of your salvation" is?

After they heard the "Word of truth," what did they do?

What did they receive?

What verb is used to describe what happened when they received the Holy Spirit?

> DIGGING DEEPER: Sealed is the Greek word *sphragizō* which contains more than one meaning to reveal the extent to which God has gone to insure our understanding of what sealed really means. One meaning is "to set a seal upon, to seal for security from satan." Since we are born again in our spirit, being sealed shows us that there is a seal upon our spirit that forbids satan's access. Another aspect of the word sealed is used "in order to prove, confirm or authenticate a thing. To prove one's testimony to a person that he is what he professes to be." This means that at the moment we heard the gospel – the good news – and believed and received it as truth we were vacuum packed with the Holy Spirit of promise. Vine's Expository Dictionary confirms this by explaining that God marked with a seal those who have received the Holy Spirit indicating who belong to Him. The Holy Spirit living in our spirit is a testimony to satan of his defeat and to ourselves of God's great love and presence in our lives. That is how much God loves his children, he wouldn't even let us go it alone after we made a decision to following Him.

V14 From the KJV, what is the Holy Spirit?

What word does AOV use for "earnest"?

Until what happens?   Of what?

V15 What was it that Paul heard about the Ephesians? (pick all that apply)
- That they were complaining about the coffee served at church.
- That their evangelism numbers were increasing.
- Of their faith in the Lord Jesus.
- Of their love for God's people.

V16 What two things did Paul do because of what he had heard about the Ephesians?
1.
2.

The words **in Christ, in him, and in whom** are listed 9 times in Ephesians 1:1-16. Read through this portion of scripture and highlight them on your KJV scripture sheet.

Write in the Notes section or on a separate sheet of paper what each scripture is saying in relation to the statements **in Christ, in him or in whom**.

DIGGING DEEPER: The words "in Christ" are mentioned 40 times in the New Testament. Paul, the writer of the majority of the New Testament, must have had a very clear understanding of what it means to be in Christ. When God looks at us he sees us "in Christ" through our born again spirit that is filled with Jesus through the Holy Spirit. In our born again spirits we are washed clean by the blood of Jesus. God does not see our impurities, faults, or junk, he sees Jesus. This is why we need to get our body and soul (mind, will and emotions) conformed to Christ who already lives in us.

Paul shows in this section of Ephesians some of the spiritual blessings that are ours because we are in Christ. Highlight or underline them on the KJV scripture sheet.

V3 We have received all spiritual blessings that originate in the heavenlies where Christ is seated at the right hand of God.

V4 We have been chosen to be holy and blameless in right standing before him. Love did this!

V5 Jesus Christ was planned from the very beginning. God's purpose was to adopt mankind through what Jesus Christ did.

V6 We are beloved of God because of what Jesus has done.

V7 We have been redeemed (bought back) and our sins have been forgiven.

V8 We have all wisdom and understanding. Whose wisdom and understanding do we have? God's.

V11 We have received an inheritance. There are 7,000 in the Word.

V13 After we believed, we received a portion of that inheritance, which is the Holy Spirit.

SCRIPTURE - WORKSHEET 2
Ephesians 1:17 – 2:5

¹⁷ that the God of our Lord Jesus Christ, the Father of glory, may give unto you the spirit of wisdom and revelation in the knowledge of him:

¹⁸ the eyes of your understanding being enlightened; that ye may know what is the hope of his calling, and what the riches of the glory of his inheritance in the saints,

¹⁹ and what *is* the exceeding greatness of his power to us-ward who believe, according to the working of his mighty power,

²⁰ which he wrought in Christ, when he raised him from the dead, and set *him* at his own right hand in the heavenly *places*,

²¹ far above all principality, and power, and might, and dominion, and every name that is named, not only in this world, but also in that which is to come:

²² and hath put all *things* under his feet, and gave him *to be* the head over all *things* to the church,

²³ which is his body, the fulness of him that filleth all in all.

2 And you *hath he quickened*, who were dead in trespasses and sins;

² wherein in time past ye walked according to the course of this world, according to the prince of the power of the air, the spirit that now worketh in the children of disobedience:

³ among whom also we all had our conversation in times past in the lusts of our flesh, fulfilling the desires of the flesh and of the mind; and were by nature the children of wrath, even as others.

⁴ But God, who is rich in mercy, for his great love wherewith he loved us,

⁵ even when we were dead in sins, hath quickened us together with Christ, (by grace ye are saved;)

Worksheet 2
Ephesians 1:17–2:5

Read Ephesians 1:17-2:5 everyday and prior to completing this worksheet.

V17 In V16 Paul says that he mentions the Ephesians in what?

Paul is going to tell us what he prays for people whom he has heard what two things about? (V15)
1.
2.

Paul uses two descriptions for God, what are they?
1.
2.

Complete this sentence: "may give unto you the _____ of _____ and _____ in the _____ of _____."

Is the word "spirit" speaking of the Holy Spirit or man's spirit?

Doesn't **verse 8** say they already had wisdom? Yes or No

Where did the wisdom from **V8** come from? Learning, Mankind, or God.

In **verse 17**, Paul prays for the Ephesians to have wisdom and revelation in what?

Paul prays for them to have wisdom and knowledge of whom?

DIGGING DEEPER: What "spirit" is supposed to have wisdom and revelation? Didn't Paul just say in verse 9 that believers had been given wisdom and now he is praying for these believers to get the spirit of wisdom and revelation. Is this a little confusing? Let's see if we can shed a little light on this by looking at the word spirit.
  Strong's Exhaustive Concordance divides "spirit" into 3 categories: Human, superhuman and divine.
1. Divine: Is God the Holy Spirit and Christ's Spirit.
2. Superhuman: Are angels and demons.(Having capabilities beyond human)
3. Human: Which is man's rational soul or mental disposition.

Mental disposition is the way we act and think. We know that the bible says that man also is a spirit because that is where we house Christ and the Holy Spirit. (1 Thess. 5:23, Heb 4:12, Gal. 4:6 just to name a few.) **continued on next page...**

> According to Strong's Exhaustive Concordance the word "wisdom" is *sophia* in the Greek. It means "broad or full of intelligence; used of the knowledge of very diverse matters." Colossians 2:2-3 tells us that all the treasures of wisdom and knowledge are hid in God and Christ. The Spirit that is of God and Christ already possesses wisdom and knowledge.
>
> Reading on in Colossians 2 we see that we are complete in Him or in Christ. The only way that we are complete in Him is through our born again spirits. Therefore, that wisdom and knowledge is resident in our born again spirits (V8) because we received it as a package deal at salvation. Even though we have these in us because of the indwelling of the Holy Spirit, we have to work through our mental disposition to live it out of our soul (mind, will, emotions).
>
> Paul's prayer is that believers will get a revelation of what their born again spirits already possess because of the completed work of Jesus, so that their mental disposition will be lived out of their born again spirits. Paul goes on to say that this is accomplished through a revealing of the "knowledge of God." This Greek word for "knowledge" is *ginosko* which is not a mere knowing of God but an intimate, experiential knowledge relationship. That would mean that you know Him so well that if someone tried to tell you something that was not true about Him you would know it right away.

V18 Paul wants the "eyes" of the Ephesians what to be enlightened?

> DIGGING DEEPER: What are the "eyes of our understanding"? Some translations use the word <u>heart</u> for the word understanding. According to the Greek root words it should actually say "through the mind, thoughts or imaginations." Paul is telling believers that the way they think or imagine has to be illuminated or become clearer in the knowledge of God's call on their life and the richness of the inheritance God has placed in the saints or in believers.
>
> God is so wonderful that he left us his Word so we can discover His personality and understand the fullness of His love for us expressed through Jesus. I suggest reading the Word as if you haven't read it before starting with everything about Jesus. Jesus Christ is the true revelation of the Father, not the situations of the bible or even the circumstances of our lives.

Paul wants this so that they will know three things, name the first one listed:

Look up the word "hope" in any source and give its meaning:

Whose calling is Paul talking about?

What is the second thing Paul wants the Ephesians to know?

Look up the word "riches" in any source and give its meaning:

Who is the "his" in this statement?

What is it that is his?

Where is this inheritance?

Do you have this inheritance? Yes or No How do you know?

V19 There is one more thing Paul wants the Ephesians to know, what is that?

The "his" in this verse is referring to this power belonging to whom?

Who is this power going to or toward?

Who would <u>not</u> be included in receiving this power?

The phrase "according to" in this verse means "in keeping with or in agreement with." This power that believers receive is "in agreement with" what?
KJV

AOV

Can you give some examples of what God's power working through believers has already done? (Try to list at least two)
1.
2.

DIGGING DEEPER: There are three important things that Paul lists here that we will experience by having the wisdom and revelation of the knowledge of God illuminated to us.
1. <u>The hope of His calling.</u> Vine's Expository Dictionary best describes the hope of his calling as "God's invitation to man to accept the benefits of salvation." When we examine the meaning of the word salvation we find it encompasses more than a one time event. It speaks of deliverance, restoration, health, wholeness. Living life in the fullness of what Jesus purchased with his death, burial and resurrection.

> 2. <u>The riches of the glory of His inheritance in the saints.</u> An inheritance is everything that belonged to a relative and because the relative is no longer humanly alive those who are the heir or living relatives mentioned in the will are entitled to the inheritance. The inheritance is demonstrated to us by what Jesus Christ has done and is demonstrated by us because Jesus Christ lives in and through us by His Holy Spirit.
> 3. <u>The exceeding greatness of His power to us-ward who believe.</u> The remainder of verse 19 goes on to clarify the power that is used by the believer who is in Christ. It is God's power that is at work behind the scenes that is working through us. That same, identical power that raised Jesus from the dead. That same, identical power that seated Jesus at the right hand of the Father past all principalities, powers, mights and dominions. That same, identical power is at work through us if we will remain in Him, believe, and use it.

V20 What was it that was "wrought or at work" in Christ?

There are two things listed here that the power of God did in Christ. Name the first one:
1.

Write below how you would explain to someone what it means to "raise someone from the dead." (Make it so simple that a child could understand it)

What is the second thing listed that the power of God did in Christ?
2.

Whose power did these things?

According to verse 19, where is this power at this present time?

V21 According to this verse, is this power under, below, level with, above or far above all things?

Paul lists a breakdown of the entities that this power is far above. List them below:
1.
2.
3.
4.
5.

Is the above list of entities for or against God?

In your opinion, would God use his power to further these or destroy them?

Read Colossians 2:15 What did Christ do to these principalities and powers?

> DIGGING DEEPER: This verse is one of the most descriptive scriptures in the Bible as to the utter defeat of satan and all of his demonic entities. Looking closely at the action words in this verse will explain with more clarity the absolute effectiveness of what Jesus accomplished by his death, burial, and resurrection. When the Greek meanings are incorporated in the description of what Paul is saying it could be read as *"Wholly putting off and disarming principalities and powers, a public example was made of them, visible to all present, celebrated by a triumphant procession displaying Christ's complete victory."* We who are in Christ and believe in what Jesus Christ accomplished for us can live in this victory.

Back to Ephesians 1:19 According to this verse, where is this power at this present time?

Pick from the following all that apply regarding this power:
- This power could only be used when Christ was on earth.
- This power can be used by everybody, at anytime.
- This power is God's power.
- This power is now in believers who have Christ in them.
- This power is far above things in this world.
- This power does not work on situations I encounter in my life.
- Things of this world are far below this power.
- Things in the future are far below this power.
- This is the same power Jesus used to defeat the enemy and set people free when he walked the earth.
- This same power is in me. (Say it out Loud!!)

V22 The "his" and "him" in this verse is referring to whom? (v20 gives a clue)

What two things did God do in Christ?
1.
2.

How many things are under Christ's feet?

God made Christ the head over how many things?

For whose benefit did God do these two things in Christ?

In your opinion, who or what is the church?

V23 Who is the "his" and "him" in this verse?

Who is "his" body?

Paul says the church is what?

Look up the word "fullness" and give its meaning:

Read John 1:1 What was in the beginning?

This Word was two things at the beginning. What are they?
1.
2.

Read John 1:14 What happened to the Word?

Read John 1:16 What is it that we have received?

Personally, for you, what does it mean to you to be the fullness of Christ or what does that fullness of Christ look like in your life?

> DIGGING DEEPER: What is this fullness that we have as the church of believers? The Greek word used for "fullness" is *pleroma*. Strong's Exhaustive Concordance gives a meaning relevant to the New Testament use of this word. It says this fulness is "the body of believers, as that which is filled with the presence, power, agency, riches of God and of Christ." We should always be aware that every time we minister God's love, compassion, healing, and deliverance to someone, we release the fullness of God out of us to touch a person or situation.

Ephesians 2:1 Who is the "you" in this verse?

Does this verse indicate something present or past?

What were these people?

Read Ephesians 1:20 Was Christ dead at one time? Yes or No

What happened to Christ?

Back to Ephesians 2:1 Now what has Christ done for us who were also dead?

Look up the meaning of the word "quickened" and write it below:

V2 What time period is this scripture talking about?

Is this scripture for all Christians, only the Ephesians or only those who received the letter in Paul's day?

This verse shows what happened before believers knew Christ. Write below the three things that influenced believers prior to knowing Christ:
1.
2.
3.

What did Paul call the being who rules this world?
KJV _____ AOV _____

Where is this power at work now?

In your opinion, who are the children of disobedience?

V3 Who would the "we all" be in this verse?

Is this verse talking about the past, present or future?

How does the KJV list how we lived our lives in the past?
1.
2.

How does AOV list how we lived our lives in the past?
1.
2.

What does each bible version say these children were?
KJV_____ AOV _____

Are you children of wrath or punishment now? Yes or No Give a reason for your answer?

V4 God was rich in what, according to this verse?

God loved us with what, according this verse?

V5 When was it that God loved us?
    When we were perfect.
    When we were forgiven from all our sins.
    When we were going to church.
    When we were dead in sin or in the middle of doing wrong.

What did God do when we were dead in sin?
KJV
AOV

Did God do this because we earned it by our actions or anything that we had done? Yes or No

How could this have happened: when we were children of punishment, deserving of God's wrath and committing sins, then we were made alive with Christ? Write out below the words in parentheses from the KJV of **verse 5**:

Explain as best you can what that phrase "by grace ye are saved" means:

DIGGING DEEPER: **Verses 2:1,2,3**
These verses are talking about the children of disobedience which is what we all were before we put our trust in Christ. Notice how Paul isn't indecisive about whether or not some of us walked in the ways of the world and some of us didn't. It is very clear that if you are not born again and serving God, you are serving the devil by default. 2 Corinthians 4:4 says that "the god of this world hath blinded the minds of them which believe not, lest the light of the glorious gospel of Christ ...should shine on them." One aspect of my prayer for those who do not believe is that the blindness will be taken off their minds so that they can see the true light of the glorious gospel of Christ. And then, I tell them the gospel. They can't believe in something that they haven't heard. And how will they hear without someone telling them of the good news of Jesus.

SCRIPTURE - WORKSHEET 3
Ephesians 2:6 – 2:22

⁶ and hath raised *us* up together, and made *us* sit together in heavenly *places* in Christ Jesus:

⁷ that in the ages to come he might shew the exceeding riches of his grace in *his* kindness toward us through Christ Jesus.

⁸ For by grace are ye saved through faith; and that not of yourselves: *it is* the gift of God:

⁹ not of works, lest any man should boast.

¹⁰ For we are his workmanship, created in Christ Jesus unto good works, which God hath before ordained that we should walk in them.

¹¹ Wherefore remember, that ye *being* in time past Gentiles in the flesh, who are called Uncircumcision by that which is called the Circumcision in the flesh made by hands;

¹² that at that time ye were without Christ, being aliens from the commonwealth of Israel, and strangers from the covenants of promise, having no hope, and without God in the world:

¹³ but now in Christ Jesus ye who sometimes were far off are made nigh by the blood of Christ.

¹⁴ For he is our peace, who hath made both one, and hath broken down the middle wall of partition *between us;*

¹⁵ having abolished in his flesh the enmity, *even* the law of commandments *contained* in ordinances; for to make in himself of twain one new man, *so* making peace;

¹⁶ and that he might reconcile both unto God in one body by the cross, having slain the enmity thereby:

¹⁷ and came and preached peace to you which were afar off, and to them that were nigh.

¹⁸ for through him we both have access by one Spirit unto the Father.

¹⁹ Now therefore ye are no more strangers and foreigners, but fellow citizens with the saints, and of the household of God;

²⁰ and are built upon the foundation of the apostles and prophets, Jesus Christ himself being the chief corner*stone;*

²¹ in whom all the building fitly framed together groweth unto an holy temple in the Lord:

²² in whom ye also are builded together for an habitation of God through the Spirit.

Worksheet 3
Ephesians 2:6 - 22
Read Ephesians 2:6-22 daily and prior to completing this worksheet.

V6 From **verse 4**, who is the being that has performed what this verse says?

From **verses 5 and 6** there are three things that God did for us <u>together</u> in Christ. Name them:
1.
2.
3.

Christ is raised to where?

Where is Christ seated?

Read Ephesians 1:20 More specifically, where is Christ seated?

Ephesians 2:6 Is this verse telling us that at this very moment, we are also made alive, raised up and seated where Christ is? Yes or No

Read Colossians 3:1 What are we supposed to do because of our position in Christ or because of who Christ has made us?

Try to name three things that are above that we should be seeking?
1.
2.
3.

DIGGING DEEPER: "Together" mentioned 3 times in verses 5&6 are all in the Greek aorist tense which means that the events that took place <u>together</u> have already happened. This means we have been made alive when Christ was made alive, we have been raised up when Christ was raised up and we now sit together in the heavenly realm in Christ. If we tried to figure this out in some logical way our minds would probably explode. So, with steadfast faith, we accept what God has done for us in Christ and we determine to live out of that "together" where Christ is seated on the throne of power. From this throne position we access everything that Christ purchased from His death, burial, and resurrection which resides in us by the power of the Holy Spirit. Health, wholeness, healing, deliverance, as we should be.

Ephesians 2:7 This verse is God's purpose in doing those 3 things. Write out this verse below from the KJV:
_____
_____
_____
_____
_____

What does AOV use for "the ages to come"?

What words does the KJV use to describe the intensity of God's grace?

God showed this grace by what?

Through whom?

V8 Look up the meanings of the following:
By

Through

There are two things in this verse that are necessary to become saved, fill in the blanks with those things:
By _____   Through _____

Read Ephesians 3:7 Tells us about grace. Is it a gift or is it earned?

Is it of God or of man?

Read Titus 2:11 What is it that the grace of God does?

Read Romans 10:17 How does faith come?

Ephesians 2:9 What does the phrase "not of works" mean to you?

Why is it important to know that nothing man did caused him to be saved?

V10 There are two things listed here that we are because we are saved. What are they?
1.   2.

What does it mean to be someone's workmanship?

For what were we created?

Are these good works that we have decided to do or God has prepared for us to do?

Are these good works done once in a while, once a week, when we feel like it or is it how we live our daily lives?

These good works are a result of God's workmanship that is where?

When did God decide to make us his workmanship in order to house Christ Jesus?

Read Romans 9:23 What is God making known?

God's glory is being make known toward whom?

When did God decide to do this?

In your opinion, what do you think the "riches of his glory" would be?

V11 Fill in the blanks: "Wherefore _____, that ye being ____ _____ _____ _____ in _____ _____, who are called _____ by that which is _____ the _____ in the _____ _____ ___ _____;"

Who are the circumcised?

Who are the uncircumcised?

What is it that Paul wants them to remember?

V12 What time is Paul talking about at the beginning of this verse?
(v11 will give you the answer)

At that time, what were they without?

There are four things listed here that are the consequences of not having Christ in their lives, list them:
1.
2.
3.
4.

V13 What changed to make them not those four things from the last verse?

What were they before?

What has happen now because of Christ?

How did that happen?

V14 What is Jesus Christ?

There are two things that Jesus Christ our peace did, list them:
1.   2.

What two groups is this verse talking about?
        Children & Adults, You &your neighbors, Jew & Gentile.

V15 What did Christ destroy in his flesh?

Look up the word "enmity" in any source and give its meaning:

In destroying the enmity something else was also destroyed. What was that?

What was God creating in Christ by destroying the enmity and laws?

What was the ultimate result?

V16 What was Jesus' purpose for making these two people groups one?

How was this accomplished?

What was slain or killed or ended because of what was done at the cross?

V17 Is this verse still talking about what Jesus has accomplished? Yes or No?

What does this verse say that Jesus did to them?

To what two groups did he preach peace?
1.
2.

What does AOV call "the enmity"?

V18 Through Jesus, what was accomplished?
    They could all get together and build a church building.
    They could all sacrifice animals and obey laws together.
    They could all have access to the Father by one and the same Spirit.

Whose spirit gives Jew and Gentile access to the Father?

V19 The results of what the Father did through Jesus for the Jews and Gentiles are that they are no longer what?
1.   2.

But they are these two things.
1.   2.

V20 Look up the word "foundation" in any source and give its meaning:

The Ephesians foundation was built upon what?

Who was the chief cornerstone of that foundation?

V21 Who is the "whom" in this verse?

What is fitly framed or joined together in Christ?

Who does the phrase "all the building" represent?

What does the building grow into?

What was the purpose of the building called the temple in the Old Testament?

Read 1 Corinthians 3:16 Paul is talking to believers. Who is he telling them they are?

What dwells in them?

V22 Who is the whom in this verse?

They are what?

For what purpose?

Look up the word "habitation" and give its meaning:

How does this habitation of God happen?

What spirit is this verse talking about: man's spirit or God's Spirit?

DIGGING DEEPER: **ROMANS 10:17** Salvation is obtained by God's grace and received through faith. In Romans 10:17 we see that faith comes by hearing the gospel; the good news of what Jesus Christ has done for mankind. Paul mentions later in Ephesians that the way they received was to hear the gospel, believe it as truth and receive it for themselves. It is the revealing of the Word that speaks to a persons heart, that causes faith to rise in them, which enables them to receive what Christ has done. People can sit in a church their entire lives and never receive what Christ has done until that Word touches their spirit and has personal meaning to them.

DIGGING DEEPER: **FAITH** There appears to be 2 types of faith. Man's faith uses the five senses to determine whether something is believed or not. According to Romans 4:17 God's faith says that things are a certain way before they are physically seen that way. My salvation was received by me when I decided to accept Jesus as my Lord and Savior however, Jesus accomplished my salvation two-thousand years ago. My five-senses faith cannot grasp or understand how that was possible therefore I believe that God's faith, who saw it all happen, had to be present in order for me to receive. It is so reassuring for me to know that God witnessed the defeat that Jesus won for me and mankind. I can put my faith in God because he sees Jesus sitting at His right hand. God sees what Jesus has accomplished. Less pressure to perform to receive for me, all I have to do is trust.

SUMMARY CHAPTERS 1-3

Summary: Chapter 1
WHAT WE HAVE AS WE ARE **IN CHRIST**:
- V3   In Christ we partake of all spiritual blessings. On earth as it is in heaven.
- V4   In Christ we are holy and blameless as adopted children. (v5)
- V7   In Christ we have been purchased back and our sins forgiven because of His favor.
- V8   In Christ His wisdom and understanding changes us.
- V9   In Christ we know the mystery of God's good pleasure of His will.
- V10 In Christ we are gathered together as one.
- V11 In Christ we received an inheritance.
- V12 In Christ we are called a visible manifestation of God's presence.
- V13 In Christ we trusted for our salvation.
- V13 In Christ we received the seal of the Holy Spirit's presence NEVER to be removed.

Paul's prayer is to know what we have:
- V17 That we have accurate knowledge of who Christ is and what he has done in our spirits.
- V18 That we would be mindful of God's call for us & the riches of His inheritance we possess.
- V19 That we would know the power working in us as related to how it works in Christ.
- V23 That we are FULL of that power, bearing that fulness in our present lives.

Summary: Chapter 2
Paul is showing the oneness of Jew and Gentile in the word "together."
- v5,6 Together (Jew and Gentile) being given life, raised and seated with Christ.
- V10 One workmanship.
- V13 Brought together by the blood of Christ.
- V18 Access to the Father by one Spirit.
- V22 One habitation together of God through the Spirit.

Summary: Chapter 3
The Purpose of one body of believers.
- V2   Revealing the mystery of the dispensation of the grace of Christ.
- V6   That Gentiles are fellow heirs, of the same body, partakers of his promise in Christ.
- V8   Preaching the unsearchable riches of Christ.
- V9   Making all see the fellowship of this mystery.
- V10 So that the church reveals God's wisdom to the principalities and powers in the heavens.
- V11 Which was God's eternal purpose.
- V12 Having boldness and confidence to show the riches of Christ, the mystery & wisdom of God.

Showing how to accomplish the Purpose.
That the church would understand the embodiment of Christ and God's power in us:
- V16 That we would allow the Holy Spirit to strengthen our inner man.
- V17 So rooted and grounded in Christ's love that dwells in our hearts.
- V18 Having our minds fixed on the wholeness of Christ's love for us.
- V19 So that God can completely house His fulness in us.
- V20 Knowing God is able to do beyond what we ask or think by His power that works through us.

NOTES

SCRIPTURE - WORKSHEET 4
Ephesians 3:1 – 15

¹For this cause I Paul, the prisoner of Jesus Christ for you Gentiles,

²if ye have heard of the dispensation of the grace of God which is given me to you-ward:

³how that by revelation he made known unto me the mystery; (as I wrote afore in few words,

⁴whereby, when ye read, ye may understand my knowledge in the mystery of Christ)

⁵which in other ages was not made known unto the sons of men, as it is now revealed unto his holy apostles and prophets by the Spirit;

⁶that the Gentiles should be fellow heirs, and of the same body, and partakers of his promise in Christ by the gospel:

⁷whereof I was made a minister, according to the gift of the grace of God given unto me by the effectual working of his power.

⁸Unto me, who am less than the least of all saints, is this grace given, that I should preach among the Gentiles the unsearchable riches of Christ;

⁹and to make all *men* see what *is* the fellowship of the mystery, which from the beginning of the world hath been hid in God, who created all things by Jesus Christ:

¹⁰to the intent that now unto the principalities and powers in heavenly *places* might be known by the church the manifold wisdom of God,

¹¹according to the eternal purpose which he purposed in Christ Jesus our Lord:

¹²in whom we have boldness and access with confidence by the faith of him.

¹³Wherefore I desire that ye faint not at my tribulations for you, which is your glory.

¹⁴For this cause I bow my knees unto the Father of our Lord Jesus Christ,

¹⁵of whom the whole family in heaven and earth is named,

Worksheet 4
Ephesians 3:1 – 3:15

Read Ephesians 3:1 – 3:15 daily and prior to completing this worksheet.

V1 What is the first statement Paul makes in this verse, prior to stating his name?

Read Ephesians 2:19-22(you can go back further if you want) and write below how you would describe what Paul means by the statement "for this cause"?
_____
_____
_____

What does Paul call himself in this verse?

For whom is Paul a prisoner?

In what city was Paul a prisoner? (Acts 28:16)

V2 What was it that the Ephesians had heard?

Look up the word "dispensation" from any source and give its meaning:

Who was given this message?

For whom was Paul given the message?

V3 How did Paul receive this message?

Who made known this revelation message to Paul?

What does Paul call this message in each version?
KJV _____   AOV _____

Had Paul told them about this mystery before, or was this the only time?

V4 What were the Ephesians going to understand when they read what Paul had written before?

V5 Was there ever a time when this mystery was not known by the sons of men?

When was that?
KJV _____ AOV _____

Who are the "sons of men"?

Is this being revealed now as it was in Paul's day?

To whom is the mystery being revealed in this verse?

How is this mystery being revealed to them?

Read Galatians 1:12 How was this mystery made known unto Paul?

Look up the word "revelation" and give its meaning:

Ephesians 3:6 This describes the mystery that Paul is talking about. There are three main points to this mystery, write them below:
1.
2.
3.

Who is the "his" in this verse?

Where is this promise?

In your opinion, describe what you think the gospel is?

V7 Who is the "I" in this verse?

What was Paul made?

Look up the word "minister" in any source and give its meaning:

By what was Paul made a minister?

How was this gift given unto Paul?

Look up the word "effectual" in any source and give its meaning:

Is this verse saying that the gift of grace Paul received from God was given because of God's power that accomplishes what it is sent to accomplish, which in this verse is to make Paul a minister of the gospel? Yes or No

V8 How does Paul explain himself in this verse?

What was given to him?

Paul is a minster or called to preach to whom?

Is Paul a Gentile? Yes or No. If No, then what is he?

What is the message that Paul is given the grace to preach?
KJV _____ AOV _____

V9 There is more to what Paul has been called by God to do. What must he make all men see?

How long has this mystery been hidden?

Where has this mystery been hidden?

Write out the next statement about God that starts with "who"

_____
_____

Read Isaiah 44:24 Who does Isaiah say is speaking in this verse?

Who does God say created all things?

When you compare Isaiah 44:24 to Ephesians 3:9 Is Jesus Christ deity or God? Yes or No

John 1:1-3 V2 Where was the Word in the beginning?

V3 Was anything made without the Word or without Jesus? Yes or No

Ephesians 3:10 What time frame is this verse addressing? (pick all that apply) Prior to Jesus, Paul's day, After Jesus death, Old Testament times, Currently in our time.

What is it that is being made known?
KJV _____ AOV _____

Who is making this known?

The church is making this known to whom?

Who would you say are the "principalities and powers in heavenly places"?

DIGGING DEEPER: The words "principalities and powers" (P&P) in this verse are the same words that were used in Ephesians 6:12 that describes the armor we wear against these P&P. This verse says that the church will show God's manifold or multifaceted wisdom to these P&P. What is the purpose of God's wisdom being shown through the church? I believe that it is to show the P&P their utter defeat through the church walking in the fullness of what Jesus Christ has accomplished. A great majority of the church has a lack of knowledge of who they are in Christ which has caused many to walk in defeat when we are victorious through what Jesus Christ has done. We are the Winners!!! The fight has been fought. The victor has been decided. It is Jesus Christ and he lives in you. We can show the unseen realm that victory over and over again as we live our lives as Winners!! Victory is for believers who allow Christ to reign through and be King on the throne of their life. How awesome would it be to watch the unseen realm and see the dumbfounded faces on the principalities and powers as God's children walk as Winners!!!

V11 God's plan to make his wisdom known to principalities and powers through the church was according to:
- A momentary thought.
- An idea by the angels.
- A plan from the beginning of time.

This plan was accomplished through whom?

V12 Who is the "whom" this verse is talking about?

Who is the "we" this verse is talking about?

What two things does this verse say the "we" have?
1.

2.

How is the "we" able to possess those two things?

Who is the "him" in this verse?

DIGGING DEEPER: This boldness and access with confidence could be talking about our being able to approach God without the barrier of the sin nature. This is really the gospel or good news that Jesus purchased with his death, burial and resurrection. But I believe that the surrounding verses suggest something in addition to what Jesus accomplished on our behalf. Paul has just told the Gentiles that they are included as heirs of the promise and partakers of the riches of Christ. The Gentiles are now part of the church or the body of believers. In verse 10 Paul tells them that they will be displaying the multifaceted wisdom of God before the principalities and powers in the spiritual world. What would make the P&P angry? If believers would live out everything that Jesus came to bring them. I believe that the boldness is to be bold enough to expect the same things that Jesus did on earth to be done by us. (Mark 16) The confident access is that we can take all that Christ has accomplished in his defeat of the enemy and **walk all over principalities and powers** by displaying before them the Victory Christ has won.

V13 Because the "we" have boldness and confident access to God, what is it that Paul desires for them <u>NOT</u> to do? (Pick one)

Run, jump, have courage, faint, have boldness.

What phrase is used in AOV for "faint not"?

At what are "we" not to faint?

> DIGGING DEEPER: The word "faint" has the meaning of becoming weary, discouraged or exhausted. If the Ephesians would become weary because of what Paul was going through, the victory won for the kingdom, their salvation and those they would reach, would turn to be defeat. They need to keep that boldness and confidence and know that what happens in the physical world does not determine what is taking place in the spiritual world. Bringing the kingdom to earth depends on them being able to stand strong.

On behalf of whom does Paul say he goes through these things?

On behalf of what does Paul say it benefits those for whom he goes through this?

2 Corinthians 11:23-28 Name six of the things that Paul went through to bring the gospel to believers:

1.   2.
3.   4.
5.   6.

Ephesians 3:14 Paul says "For this cause" to begin this verse. To what cause is he referring? (v13)

What does Paul do because of that reason?

What do we call what Paul is doing?

To whom is Paul bowing his knee?

V15 Paul uses the words "the whole family" in this verse. Who do you think "the whole family" represents?

From where is the whole family represented?

What is it that the whole family has received?

Are you named with the same name that they have received? Yes or No

Read Philippians 2:9-11 What is the name that is higher than any other name?

What must bow to that name?
1.
2.
3.

Would what Paul is about to pray apply to you?   Yes or No

>Be sure to read and meditate on what Paul is praying from the next Worksheet. Ephesians 3:16-21

SCRIPTURE - WORKSHEET 5
Ephesians 3:16 – 4:10

¹⁶ that he would grant you, according to the riches of his glory, to be strengthened with might by his Spirit in the inner man;

¹⁷ that Christ may dwell in your hearts by faith; that ye, being rooted and grounded in love,

¹⁸ may be able to comprehend with all saints what *is* the breadth, and length, and depth, and height;

¹⁹ and to know the love of Christ, which passeth knowledge, that ye might be filled with all the fulness of God.

²⁰ Now unto him that is able to do exceeding abundantly above all that we ask or think, according to the power that worketh in us,

²¹ unto him *be* glory in the church by Christ Jesus throughout all ages, world without end. Amen.

4 I therefore, the prisoner of the Lord, beseech you that ye walk worthy of the vocation wherewith ye are called,

² with all lowliness and meekness, with longsuffering, forbearing one another in love;

³ endeavouring to keep the unity of the Spirit in the bond of peace.

⁴ *There is* one body, and one Spirit, even as ye are called in one hope of your calling;

5 one Lord, one faith, one baptism,

⁶ one God and Father of all, who *is* above all, and through all, and in you all.

⁷ But unto every one of us is given grace according to the measure of the gift of Christ.

⁸ Wherefore he saith, When he ascended up on high, he led captivity captive, and gave gifts unto men.

⁹ (Now that he ascended, what is it but that he also descended first into the lower parts of the earth?

¹⁰ He that descended is the same also that ascended up far above all heavens, that he might fill all things.)

Worksheet 5
Ephesians 3:16 – 4:10

Read Ephesians 3:16 – 4:10 daily and prior to completing this worksheet.

V16 Who is the "he" in this verse?

Who is the "you" in this verse?

Paul is praying "according to" or based on what?

What would you think the statement "according to the riches of his glory" means?

What does Paul desire for them to be?

What is the source of this might or power?

Where does Paul desire this to happen?

Read 2 Corinthians 4:16 This verse is speaking about two parts of a man. List them below:
1.
2.
Next to each part of man above, write what is happening to each, according to this verse.

What man is Paul talking about in **Ephesians 3:16**?

DIGGING DEEPER: Having an understanding of the 3 parts of human beings is essential to understanding what happened at the born again experience and to better understand what Paul desires for believers. We are spirit, soul and body. Our spirit is what was renewed at the new birth or born again experience. Our spirit is now 100% Jesus by way of the Holy Spirit. However, that does not automatically change our thinking or our actions because we also possess a soul, which this verse refers to as the inner man. Our soul is where we think, reason, make decisions, and experience feelings. Our soul has been influenced by the world up to the point at which we decided to ask Jesus to be our Lord and Savior. Our soul learned everything based on self-focused survival by worldly ways. Finally, we all have a body (obvious, Huh!) which is directly controlled by our soul.

> We have always been soul-controlled worldly beings, allowing the 5 senses to influence how we think, feel or make decisions. After Jesus becomes a part of our lives, we now have a longing for a deeper relationship with God. Unfortunately, that deeper relationship is not automatic because of our soul-controlled past way of life. Now that thinker, feeler, chooser soul needs to be renewed to the new person or inner man that we really have become. 2 Timothy 3:16 tells us that the Word of God is where we get the instructions on how to live as this new person. Because the old man had many years to perfect it's soul-controlled worldly ways, it will take time in meditation on the truth about who we really are in Christ, to change our thinking, feeling and the choices we make.
>
> Now the soul needs to think from the perspective of the finished work of Jesus Christ. This is Paul's desire for the believers in this prayer. That they would know who they really are and what they really have based on what God did through Jesus Christ on their behalf. Praise God that we can receive the benefits of this same prayer.

Ephesians 3:17 Where does Paul pray that Christ would dwell?

How does Paul pray that Christ would dwell in their hearts?

How would you describe to someone what "faith" is?

Does Christ already dwell in the believer? Yes or No

If yes, then in what part of the believer does Christ dwell?

Give a reason why Paul would pray that Christ would dwell in them if Christ already dwells in the believer?

Complete this statement "that _____, being _____ and _____ in _____."

In your opinion, what do each of the words below mean:
Rooted   _____
Grounded _____

V18 What does Paul pray for them to be able to do?

Look up the word "comprehend" in any source and give its meaning:

Who else does Paul include that are able to comprehend?

Paul lists four areas of what he desires them to comprehend. List them below:
1. _____ 2. _____
3. _____ 4. _____

V19 Pick which best describes what Paul is praying in verses 18 & 19 that he desires for these people:
- To be able to live and do.
- To be able to acknowledge and say.
- To be able to comprehend and know.

What does he want them to comprehend and know?

What is the description Paul uses in regard to this love?
- It is never ending.
- It is placed in man by cupid.
- It is a warm and cozy feeling.
- It passes knowledge.

Paul says that by comprehending and knowing the love of Christ the result would be what?

So, if we Christians want to be filled with God's fullness, then these verses tell us that we must have an understanding and knowledge of Christ's love?
   Yes or No

V20 Who do you think the "him" is in this verse? (v14 is a hint)

Paul uses two verbs to describe what the Father can do. Give their meanings:
exceeding:

abundantly:

Is what "he" can do between, below or above according to this verse?

What can "he" do exceeding and abundantly above?

65

He does this according to what?
- According to how the worlds economy is going at the time.
- According to what the government says.
- According to the power that works in us.

Where is this power?

As best you can explain where we got this power?

V21 Fill in the blanks: "Unto _____ be _____ in the _____ by _____ _____ throughout all _____, _____ without _____. _____."

Where is this glory?

How does the church make known this glory?

How long will the church be making this glory known?
KJV _____ AOV _____

> **DIGGING DEEPER:** By taking into account the Greek meanings of the words in Paul's prayer, we can have a better idea of what Paul was saying to believers.
> V16 "To us it has been granted, based on the wealth of God's presence, to be strengthened with power and ability through Hs Spirit in our inner man, V17 That the reality that Christ dwells in our spirit will become a reality in our soul, V18 That we comprehend and take possession of the depths of God's love for us and through us. V19 So that we can have experienced knowledge of Christ's love, which isn't based on common knowledge but the experience of God's fullness; all of His blessings, resources and wisdom. V20 So that we would know what God is able to do that which is exceeding abundantly above what we could ever think or ask, all experienced by the power that works in us, which is Christ's power in us."
> The only way the power of God works in and through us is if we allow it to work. If there is not power working in us; in our personal daily lives, there will be no power of God coming through us.

Chapter 4 V1 What does Paul call himself in this verse?

What does Paul encourage the readers of this letter to do?
KJV _____
AOV _____

Which statement would best describe how believers are to live?
> The same way they did before Christ came to live in them.
> As people who honor what God has done for them by their actions.

V2 Paul lists four ways that will enable the church to live worthy of the call of God. List them below:

KJV	AOV
1.	1.
2.	2.
3.	3.
4.	4.

V3 What is it that Paul asks the readers to make every effort to keep?

What Spirit is Paul talking about? Our spirit or the Holy Spirit.

How is this unity kept or continued in believers lives?
KJV _____ AOV _____

Who do you think this peace is between?

V4 & 5 Paul is making statements of truths or absolutes that are essential to the unity of the church, Christ's body. List them below:
1.
2.
3.
4.
5.
6.

V6 What is the last statement of truth or absolute that Paul mentions?

Where does this verse state that this absolute resides?
1.
2.
3.

V7 What is given unto us?

How would you explain to someone what "grace is" ?

This grace that we have been given is in regards to what?
  How many commandments we obey.
   How often we forgive others.
  The measure of the gift of Christ.

How much did you receive of Christ? (Pick one.) A little, just enough to get by, everything we need for every situation we will ever encounter.

V8 Read Psalm 68:18. What are the three things listed here that Christ did?
1.
2.
3.

The last portion of this verse tells why these three things were done. What does it say?

Ephesians 4:9 & 10 This phrase gives more description regarding the quote from Psalm 68:18.

Who is the "he" in these verses?

What happened first before he ascended?

To where did he descend?

Read 1 Peter 3:19 & 4:6
V19 What does Peter call the place that Paul called the "lower parts of the earth?" (pick one) A palace, a home, a prison, a resting place?

1 Peter 4:6 What did Jesus do while he was in that place, to those who were there?

Peter gives two reasons why the gospel needed to be preached to those in that prison or the lower part of the earth. List them below:
1.
2.

Read John 5:24-29
V28 Where does this verse say that Jesus will preach or where will they hear his voice? On earth, in the synagogue, in churches, in the graves. (pick one)

V29 There are two types of resurrection listed that the hearers will be a part of. List them below:
1.
2.

Go back to Ephesians 4:10 How far did Jesus ascend?

What reason did Paul give for Jesus descending and ascending?

Look up the word "fill" in any source and give its meanings:

During this week: Pray the prayer that Paul prayed for the Ephesians (3:16-21) with thankfulness, for someone in your life. Pray for a different person or more than one, every day. Be sure to journal who you prayed for this week so you can have a praise report to share with other believers.

SCRIPTURE - WORKSHEET 6
Ephesians 4:11-27

¹¹ And he gave some, apostles; and some, prophets; and some, evangelists; and some, pastors and teachers;

¹² for the perfecting of the saints, for the work of the ministry, for the edifying of the body of Christ:

¹³ till we all come in the unity of the faith, and of the knowledge of the Son of God, unto a perfect man, unto the measure of the stature of the fulness of Christ:

¹⁴ that we *henceforth* be no more children, tossed to and fro, and carried about with every wind of doctrine, by the sleight of men, *and* cunning craftiness, whereby they lie in wait to deceive;

¹⁵ but speaking the truth in love, may grow up into him in all things, which is the head, *even* Christ:

¹⁶ from whom the whole body fitly joined together and compacted by that which every joint supplieth, according to the effectual working in the measure of every part, maketh increase of the body unto the edifying of itself in love.

¹⁷ This I say therefore, and testify in the Lord, that ye henceforth walk not as other Gentiles walk, in the vanity of their mind,

¹⁸ having the understanding darkened, being alienated from the life of God through the ignorance that is in them, because of the blindness of their heart:

¹⁹ who being past feeling have given themselves over unto lasciviousness, to work all uncleanness with greediness.

²⁰ But ye have not so learned Christ;

²¹ if so be that ye have heard him, and have been taught by him, as the truth is in Jesus:

²² that ye put off concerning the former conversation the old man, which is corrupt according to the deceitful lusts;

²³ and be renewed in the spirit of your mind;

²⁴ and that ye put on the new man, which after God is created in righteousness and true holiness.

²⁵ Wherefore putting away lying, speak every man truth with his neighbour: for we are members one of another.

²⁶ Be ye angry, and sin not: let not the sun go down upon your wrath:

²⁷ neither give place to the devil.

Worksheet 6
Ephesians 4:11-27

Read Ephesians 4:11-27 daily and prior to completing this worksheet.

V11 From the last worksheet, we know that God has given the church gifts. There are five listed here:

1.
2.
3.
4.
5.

V12 There are three benefits for these gifts. List them below:

1. _____
   _____
2. _____
   _____
3. _____
   _____

Next to each benefit above, explain in your own words what you think each means.

Who is being equipped or perfected to minister and edify the body of Christ? Mankind, Angels, Believers, Unbelievers, Saints. (Pick all that apply)

V13 There are two results that this perfecting is to accomplish. List them below:
1.
2.

These two results will create what type of man?

The remainder of this verse describes what that type of man is. Is he:
Just starting to grow, Partially grown but have a long way to go or Fully grown.

What measure does AOV say is used to show this full growth?

Look at Ephesians 3:16-19
In Paul's prayer for the Ephesians, he wants them to be strengthened by the Spirit, to know that Christ dwells in them, to be rooted and grounded in love, and to be able to comprehend and know the love of Christ so that what can happen in them?

When that prayer is compared with **Ephesians 4:13** what is the end result that Paul wants the Ephesians and the saints to know?

V14 This verse explains what happens to believers who do <u>not</u> know for themselves that end result. What does it say they are:
                    Beggars,   sinners,   children,   saints.

What word does AOV use for the previous answer?

The KJV lists four traits of this type of person. List them below:
1.
2.
3.
4.

What does the KJV say that people are trying to do, by these traits, to others?
    Have faith in God.
     Grow in the knowledge of what Christ has done for us.
    Lie in wait to deceive.

V15 What are the saints or believers suppose to speak?

From this verse, what is the truth?

What does it cause believers to do when they speak the truth in love?

This verse says we are to grow into what?

This verse says that Christ is what?

Read Colossians 2:19. Who would Christ be in this verse?

There are three things listed here that the head does for the body, what are they?
1.
2.
3.

Because of what this verse says, can we conclude that everything that a believer needs to live life, have unity with other saints and be filled with God's fullness, comes from the head?   Yes or No

V16 This verse is describing who as the head? (from V15)

What grows from the head?

Write Verse 16 from AOV: _____
_____
_____
_____

This verse is talking about the body of Christ growing. True or False

Does each part of the body need to work in order for the body to grow?

When every part of the body is effectually working what is edified or built up?   Others that meet the body or the body itself?

What does the body of Christ have to do to grow?

V17 Paul is telling believers not to live life as whom?

V17, 18, 19 Next to each breakdown of the traits of other Gentiles below, write the equivalent from AOV.
1. "the vanity of their mind" _____
2. "having the understanding" _____
3. "alienated from the life of God through ignorance" _____
_____

4. "the blindness of their heart" _____
5. "being past feeling" _____
6. "given over to lasciviousness" _____
7. "work all uncleaness with greediness" _____

V20 Who is the "ye" or "you" in this verse?

Who does this verse say that they did not learn the things in verse 17, 18, 19 from?

V21 This verse lists two ways in which they have learned from Christ. List them below:
1.   2.

What is in Christ?

If you need to know what things are truth, where would you look?

Look up the word "truth" or "true" in any source and give its meaning.

John 8:31-32 "Then said Jesus to those Jews which believed on him, 'If ye continue in my word, *then* are ye my disciples indeed; And ye shall know the truth, and the truth shall make you free.'"

From the verses above, what did Jesus say that disciples do to show they are disciples?

What is gained by continuing in or abiding in the word?

What does knowledge of the truth do?

If we know people who are not free, what are they lacking?

V22 From the following portions of this verse write the same from AOV:
1. "put off" _____
2. "former conversation" _____
3. "the old man" _____
4. "corrupt" _____
5. "deceitful lusts" _____

When were you that old man?

V23 What needs to happen to put off that former way of life?
Be reborn, be redeemed, be received, be renewed, be righteous.

Where does this renewal take place?

V24 From the following portions of this verse write the same from AOV:
1. "put on" _____
2. "new man" _____
3. "which after God is created" _____
4. "righteousness" _____
5. "true holiness" _____

Who was your new person created to be like?

How did **verse 23** say we are to put on this new person?
1. By praying morning, noon and night.   2. By showing love to others.
3. By renewing our minds.   4. Being involved in the church.

In your opinion, to what do believers renew their minds?

Write below ways in which you renew your mind?

V25 This scripture begins Paul's examples of practical applications of the new man. To whom would these apply?

What is the first thing Paul says to "put away"?

What is the opposite or right way to handle the first thing Paul mentions?

Where does truth come from? (**V21**)

What reason does Paul give for this practical application?

Who would be the neighbor that Paul is talking about?

V26 What is the next practical application?

Is this commanding us to be angry or not be angry?

Read Psalm 97:10. What are we to hate or have intense dislike for?

In your opinion, at whom should our anger be directed?

At whom should our anger <u>not</u> be directed?

I we are ever angry, we should only be angry at the following?
(Pick all that apply)
Demons, your neighbor, the sales clerk, your spouse, evil, injustice, satan.

Ephesians 4:26 Are we ever to sin?   Yes or No

What happens when the sun goes down?
   Our human bodies want to relax.
   It is time for human bodies to rest.
   Human bodies sleep.

The KJV says "let not" at the beginning of this phrase, what does AOV say?

Who is responsible to let or not let something to happen in your life?

If a Christian were to relax or allow his anger against the enemy, the devil, to sleep, would it be possible for the devil to get an open door or influence into a Christian's life and that influence might cause them to forget who they are or sin in some area?

Ephesians 4:27 What does AOV say for the words "neither give place" from the KJV?

To whom are we <u>not</u> to give place?

In your opinion, which of the following would give place to the devil?
> Holding on to an offense.
> Being angry with a neighbor or family member.
> Degrading or speaking bad about yourself or someone else.
> Being fearful, anxious or worried about things.
> Allowing strife or conflict with others in our lives.

Give at least two ways in which you can guard yourself this week from giving place to the devil:

1.

2.

DIGGING DEEPER: <u>Understanding Anger</u> This portion of scripture seems to be very misunderstood. I read many commentaries that seem to take verse 26 out of context to get a meaning. While the common interpretation that you shouldn't go to bed angry is a great idea, the 2nd Commandment that Jesus brought us says to love your neighbor as yourself and says nothing about being angry for one day.

If we would look at verse 31 we would see a contradiction to this verse. Verse 31 tells us not to be angry. So, am I to be angry until 9 pm. or do I put anger and wrath away from me? Let's look at some scripture to help us get a clearer understanding about anger.

According to Vines Expository Dictionary regarding the word "anger" used in verse 26, it is a verb that refers to having "a just occasion for the feeling." This is a quote from Psalm 4:4 where the Hebrew word signifies "to quiver with strong emotion." This is an anger that we are suppose to have. This is righteous anger. Jesus had this same kind of anger in Mark 3:5. What made Jesus angry was the hardness of the hearts of the Pharisees. Jesus was purely perfect and never committed sin, so this anger is not related to being in sin.

The statement after the colon (:) should read "don't let your anger sleep" which explains being angry and not sinning. Paul is speaking about an anger that we are to have against evil. We are to always keep this righteous anger active against the devil and his devices. We should never let this type of anger sleep. We cannot be passive when it comes to the devil. If our anger against the devil were to rest or let down it's guard, we would open up a door and allow the enemy to have influence in our lives.

Verse 27 further confirms that if we let our guard down we would be giving place to the devil. James 4:7 tells us that our submission to God is resistance to the devil. That's why it is so important to be determined with righteous anger to keep our mind renewed to our new life with God. If we are living out the Word of God in our lives, we ARE actively fighting against evil.

SCRIPTURE - WORKSHEET 7
Ephesians 4:28 – 5:14

28 Let him that stole steal no more: but rather let him labour, working with *his* hands the thing which is good, that he may have to give to him that needeth.

29 Let no corrupt communication proceed out of your mouth, but that which is good to the use of edifying, that it may minister grace unto the hearers.

30 And grieve not the holy Spirit of God, whereby ye are sealed unto the day of redemption.

31 Let all bitterness, and wrath, and anger, and clamour, and evil speaking, be put away from you, with all malice:

32 and be ye kind one to another, tenderhearted, forgiving one another, even as God for Christ's sake hath forgiven you.

5 Be ye therefore followers of God, as dear children;

2 and walk in love, as Christ also hath loved us, and hath given himself for us an offering and a sacrifice to God for a sweet smelling savour.

3 But fornication, and all uncleanness, or covetousness, let it not be once named among you, as becometh saints;

4 neither filthiness, nor foolish talking, nor jesting, which are not convenient: but rather giving of thanks.

5 For this ye know, that no whoremonger, nor unclean person, nor covetous man, who is an idolater, hath any inheritance in the kingdom of Christ and of God.

6 Let no man deceive you with vain words: for because of these things cometh the wrath of God upon the children of disobedience.

7 Be not ye therefore partakers with them.

8 For ye were sometimes darkness, but now *are ye* light in the Lord: walk as children of light:

9 (for the fruit of the Spirit *is* in all goodness and righteousness and truth;)

10 proving what is acceptable unto the Lord.

11 And have no fellowship with the unfruitful works of darkness, but rather reprove *them*.

Worksheet 7
Ephesians 4:28 - 5:14

Read Ephesians 4:28 – 5:14 daily and prior to completing this worksheet.

V28 To whom is this verse addressed?

Does a thief take or give?

Whose influence is a thief under when he takes?

What type of work does Paul tell them to do?
                Bad, mediocre, just getting by, good?

For what purpose does Paul tell them this work is to be done?

V29 Write this verse out below from AOV. (The Amplified is very descriptive.)

_____
_____
_____
_____
_____
_____
_____

According to this verse, what type of words should we be speaking?

Beside each word below write an E for edifying or a C for corrupt next to each that they apply to:

____ gossip	____ sharing faults of others	____ forgiving words
____ kind words	____ griping about work	____ encouraging words
____ mockery	____ notice and speak good	____ complaining
____ criticism	____ negative words	____ words giving hope

V30 Who is this verse talking about?

What are we <u>not</u> to do to the Holy Spirit?

Would the things listed in verses 25, 28, 29 and 31 grieve the Holy Spirit?

Look up the word "grieve" and give its meaning below:

In regards to the believer, where is the Holy Spirit?

Until what time is the believer sealed?

Have believers already been redeemed? Yes or No

Romans 8:23 What redemption is being spoken of here?

So, what part of us has been redeemed? Body, Soul, Spirit.

Ephesians 4:31 This verse lists what is to be put away or stopped in the believers life.
1.
2.
3.
4.
5.

Paul is saying in this verse, <u>not</u> to be angry and in verse 26 he says to be angry. Are there different types of anger? Yes or No
Explain your answer:

By the statement "along with every other evil" what is Paul saying that these things are?

Who is the author of evil?

V32 What three things does Paul tell us to "be"?
1.
2.
3.

To whom are we to be these things?

In what way are we supposed to do this?

How much did God forgive us in Christ?

> DIGGING DEEPER: Paul begins bringing out some specific instructions for godly living. One thing we must remember is that Paul was addressing the issues of his day, which, although great advice, at times do not apply to the issues of our day. Verse 28 is one example. Why would Paul have to tell people not to steal anymore and to get a job? In our culture, it is natural for the majority of the people to have a job. Remembering the history at the time of Paul's writing will help us to better understand why Paul has to address issues like stealing.
>
>   Ephesus, at the time of Paul's writing, was one of the most vile corrupt cities in the world. People traveled to Ephesus to partake of their many amenities from idol worship to the well-educated and scholarly imparting wisdom at the Library of Celsus. This largely populated area, with every kind of influence imaginable, would have greater probability of influenced toward of any kind of evil offered. Stealing was most likely the mode of survival for those who chose that profession. Paul's converts in Ephesus had been engaging in the common practices of their environment.
>
>   Verse 28 also gives us insight into the real purpose of having a job for the believer:. "To have to give to those in need." Since God supplies all our needs according to Mathew 6:25-34, the joy of our job would be to give. George Muller is the example of a man who believed what Jesus said in Matthew 6 and determined to help the orphaned children in Bristol, England. George Muller took God at His Word and cared for 10,024 orphans in 5 houses. He established 117 schools which offered Christian education to over 120,000 children. He never solicited funds from anyone, but completely depended on God for everything. Who is the only one who could get the glory from a life like that? GOD That's what we want our lives to show.

Chapter 5:1 Paul's previous instructions can be concluded by telling us to be what of God?

KJV _____ AOV _____

Look up the word "imitate" and give its meaning:

When we imitate God we do it in what way?

V2 How are we to live our life?

Who is our example of love?

What did he do because of his great love for mankind?

For whom did he give himself?

Finish this verse: "Hath given himself (who?_____) for us an _____ and a _____ to God for a _____ _____ _____."

What Old Testament procedure would be like this description of what Christ has done for us?
1. Lighting of candles.
2. Placing blood on the altar.
3. Washing in a bowl.
4. Burnt offering covenant.

> DIGGING DEEPER: The Greek language has five words for the different aspects of love: Friendship love, motherly love, lustful love, emotional love and what most believers have come to know as Godly love. This Godly type of love is "agape." This verse uses agape as the love we are to give to others because we are His dearly loved children. Agape only applies to the lover, in that, it is not given based on the response of the one being loved. Agape love is a choice made no matter the situation or feelings. That is why we can love our enemies, because we use God's agape love to fulfill this command.
>
> I once had someone share that they reached out to a relative with love who was living in a sinful situation. They had told this relative that they loved them but what they were doing was wrong. As I thought and prayed about this, the Lord showed me the love that he had for me when I received and accepted what he had done for me at my born again experience. All I remember from that moment was the overwhelming love that I felt. That love had no condition of my past sins or lifestyle. If God would have brought up my past the healing power of that overwhelming love would have been broken. Because of God's love, I changed my past lifestyle from the inside out.
>
> To what extent do we give agape love to others? When we bring up a person's faults as we see them (not God working on their heart), we build a wall between those who need to experience the same unconditional love we have experienced. Did Jesus take every sin upon himself so that there is an open door to a loving relationship with the Father? Yes. Sin is not a problem for God because he took it out of the way. The love we show to others needs to be so brilliant that we can't see the wrongs they have done, but we see a hurting heart searching for the unconditional love of a Father who was willing to risk it all for them. We want them to desire what we have, not be further hurt by our love/condemnation. It is God's goodness that will lead people to see the error of their ways and repent. Romans 2:4
>
> It is not the ministry of the believer to bring up non-believers faults. While we were sinners, Christ died for us. Therefore, while they are sinners we bring the message of the good news of God's unconditional love to them. Rest assured, Romans 1:18-19 says that God is the one who shows man their unrighteousness and ungodliness. We can love them with the message of good news and let God do the rest.

V3 There are three things listed here from the KJV write the same from AOV.
Fornication _____
All uncleanness _____
Covetousness _____

Should this be talked about among believers?   Yes or No

V4 There are three things listed here from the KJV write the same from AOV.
Filthiness _____
Foolish talking _____
Jesting _____

These types of language are not acceptable or convenient for whom?

What types of words are believers supposed to say instead?

V5 There are four things here that Paul assumes that these believers already know. Write the equivalent from AOV.
Whoremonger _____
Unclean person _____
Covetous man _____
Idolater _____

All these things happen to people when they allow what to happen?
(pick one)
    When they let others lead them astray.
    When they get too busy and don't read the Word.
    When they allow things to become gods in their lives.

What is it that these people will <u>not</u> receive?

Let's look at some scriptures where Jesus talks about the Kingdom of God.
Matthew 6:33 What is the first thing Jesus tells his disciples to seek?

Matthew 12:28 What is one aspect that shows everyone that the Kingdom has come?

Mark 4:11 Does this verse imply that the parables of Jesus reveal the Kingdom of God?

Mark 10:15 How do believers receive the Kingdom of God?

In your opinion, what are some traits of little children?

Luke 7:28 Who is the greatest prophet ever born?

Who is greater than John the Baptist in the Kingdom of God?

Luke 9:2 Jesus sent the disciples to do what?

What goes along with preaching the Kingdom?

Luke 10:9 Jesus is sending out 70 disciples. What is the first thing he tells them to do?

After the sick are healed, what does Jesus tell the 70 disciples to say?

Luke 17:20-21 Jesus said the Kingdom of God is where?

DIGGING DEEPER: Signs of the Kingdom of God on the earth:
- Casting out demons – setting people free from demonic bondage.
- Healing the sick is a sign that the Kingdom has come.
- God meets our needs as we seek His Kingdom.
- Living in righteousness, peace and joy in the Holy Ghost. Romans 14:17
- Deliverance from darkness. Colossians 1:3
- Made up of children that are dependent on and trust their Father. Luke 18:16-17
- Binding and loosing are keys of the Kingdom. Matthew 16:19 Our words bind and loose: Restrain/bind what is evil, Release/loose what is good, which is the promises of the Word.
- The Kingdom of God is within the believer. Luke 17:20-21

    The religious leaders of Jesus' day were expecting the Kingdom of God to be set up like the Roman Empire that was in control at that time. They thought God would come back and take the land by godly force invading and taking over a city. The Kingdom of God's rule is within the human heart yielding to the Spirit of God within them. We bring about the Kingdom as we invade a city with love, forgiveness, healing and casting out devils, to set the captives free. Jesus has already won the victory for us. We just need to implement the benefits of the Kingdom in our daily lives.

Back to Ephesians 5:6 What does Paul warn about in this verse?

What does AOV use for "vain words"?

What comes on people who deceive in this way?

What are people called who also receive God's wrath?

In your opinion, who are these children of disobedience?

V7 What does Paul warn believers against in this verse?

Look up the word "partake" and pick the answer that best describes the meaning for this verse:
    Don't be like them.
    Don't share in what they are doing.
    Have nothing to do with them.

V8 What were the Ephesians before?

What are they now?

How are they to live or walk?

John 8:12 Who is the light?

Matthew 5:14 Who else called believers "light"?

John 9:5 What did Jesus say about who he was while on this earth?

Is that light still visible now on this earth?   Yes or No   If yes, then where?

Ephesians 5:9 What is this parenthetical phrase talking about?

Is this verse talking about man's spirit or the Holy Spirit?

Is fruit contained in a fruit tree even though it looks like the tree has no fruit at that time? Yes or No

Is the fruit of the Spirit contained in us even though we look like human beings? Yes or No

Paul lists three things that are contained in the Spirit. List them below:
1.
2.
3.

Does that mean that a Christian who has the Spirit of God living in them already has these three fruits? Yes or No

Say this out loud : "In me I have goodness, righteousness and truth."

V10 When the fruit of the Spirit listed above is walked out in a believer's life, what does this show to others?

V11 Believers are not to have fellowship with what?

The word "fellowship" is the same word for "partakers" in Revelation 18:4. In Revelation 18:4, what two things will happen to God's people if they partake of darkness?
1.
2.

In **Ephesians 5:11** what are believers to do with the unfruitful works of darkness?
KJV _____ AOV _____

V12 Fill in the blanks "For it is a (KJV) _____ (AOV) _____ to even _____ of _____ _____ which are _____ of them _____ _____."

V13 How are things reproved or revealed?

14 Christ will give light to those who are two things. What are they?
1.
2.

He tells those who sleep to do what?

He tells those who are dead to do what?

What will Christ give them?

1 John 1:7 What is the advantage to living our lives in the Light of Jesus?
1.
2.

SCRIPTURE - WORKSHEET 8
Ephesians 5:15 - 27

[15] See then that ye walk circumspectly, not as fools, but as wise,

[16] redeeming the time, because the days are evil.

[17] Wherefore be ye not unwise, but understanding what the will of the Lord *is*.

[18] And be not drunk with wine, wherein is excess; but be filled with the Spirit;

[19] speaking to yourselves in psalms and hymns and spiritual songs, singing and making melody in your heart to the Lord;

[20] giving thanks always for all things unto God and the Father in the name of our Lord Jesus Christ;

[21] submitting yourselves one to another in the fear of God.

[22] Wives, submit yourselves unto your own husbands, as unto the Lord.

[23] For the husband is the head of the wife, even as Christ is the head of the church: and he is the saviour of the body.

[24] Therefore as the church is subject unto Christ, so *let* the wives *be* to their own husbands in every thing.

[25] Husbands, love your wives, even as Christ also loved the church, and gave himself for it;

[26] that he might sanctify and cleanse it with the washing of water by the word,

[27] that he might present it to himself a glorious church, not having spot, or wrinkle, or any such thing; but that it should be holy and without blemish.

Worksheet 8
Ephesians 5:15-27

Read Ephesians 5:15–27 daily and prior to completing this worksheet.

V15 Six times in this letter Paul tells the Ephesians to "walk" or live life in certain ways. Write next to each verse below how believers are to live life:

1. **V 2:10** _____

2. **V 4:1** _____

3. **V 4:17** _____

4. **V 5:2** _____

5. **V 5:8** _____

6. **V 5:15** _____

Next to each portion of this verse write the equivalent from AOV:
"redeeming the time" _____
"the days are evil" _____

Have those evil times ended or do we still live in them?

V17 Because of what Paul says in V16 what are they <u>not</u> to do?

And what are they to do?

Look up the word "understand" in any source and give its meaning:

What is it that is to be "understood"?

Is this saying that believers should know what the Lord's will is? Yes or No

Give some examples of how we can know the Lord's will or where this information comes from:

18 What word does Paul use from the KJV to show the extent of the drunkenness of the wine drinker?

How much is an excessive amount? One drink or more than one drink.

Read Acts 2:1-4, 13-15 V4 What happened to these believers?

V13-15 What did outsiders think happened to them?

Acts 4:23-31 V31 What happened after they prayed and the house shook?

Weren't they already filled with the Holy Spirit?

What was the result from this infilling of the Holy Spirit?

Do people who have too much wine tend to be very bold? Yes or No

Could Paul be showing another aspect of being filled with the Spirit to excess? Yes or No

> DIGGING DEEPER: If we read Acts 1:8 we notice that the Holy Spirit, Jesus told the disciples to wait for, was given. Notice that the power to witness is a benefit that the Holy Spirit brings with His infilling. I see this infilling as a yielding or submitting to the work of the Holy Spirit in our lives. As Paul mentions in this verse we are to be continually filled with the Holy Spirit. As a person gets drunk with continual drinking, so we are continually filled with the Holy Spirit as we continually yield to His work in our lives being sensitive to the voice or impression of the Holy Spirit as He speaks to us. Verses 19-21 are examples Paul uses to show the process of the continual filling of the Holy Spirit. This is an excellent example of the church keeping the Holy Spirit active and present in their daily lives.

Back to Ephesians: V19, 20, 21 Paul is telling the Ephesians and believers what it looks like in their lives to be filled with the Spirit. Circle the action words at the beginning of each verse. Write them below:
19 _____ 20 _____ _____ 21 _____

V19 To whom are they to speak these things?

What are they to speak?
1.   2.   3.

What are they doing when they speak these?
1.   2.

Where do these things happen?   To whom is this all directed?

V20 What is the next thing Paul tells them to do as part of being filled with the Spirit?

How often are they to do this?

To whom do they give thanks?

In whose name do they give thanks?

V21 What is the last thing Paul tells them to do as part of being filled with the Spirit?

To whom are we to submit ourselves?

What does the phrase "in the fear of God" mean to you?

DIGGING DEEPER: Colossians 3:15-17 says, "And let the peace of God rule in your hearts, to the which also ye are called in one body; and be ye thankful. Let the word of Christ dwell in you richly in all wisdom; teaching and admonishing one another in psalms and hymns and spiritual songs, singing with grace in your hearts to the Lord. And whatsoever ye do in word or deed, do all in the name of the Lord Jesus, giving thanks to God and the Father by him."

These are parallel verses to this section of Ephesians. If we looked at Ephesians 5:20 alone we might assume that everything comes from God, good or bad, and therefore we are told by this verse, to be thankful for everything. This would contradict scriptures that speak of God being against evil. Also taking into consideration the victorious defeat Jesus won against the devil and evil, to set man free from the enemies power.

As we read the parallel verses from Colossians and compare them to Ephesians we see that the thankful attitude and affirmation is to God, our loving Father for everything HE is in our lives.

V22 Who is this verse addressing?

What are they supposed to do?   Battle, Oppose, Submit, Confront.

To whom are they submitting?

What comparison does Paul use to show us what submission to our husbands should look like?

What do you do in your life to submit to the Lord?

V23 What reason does Paul give for wives to submit to their husbands?

What comparison does Paul use to show what that type of submission looks like?

Does Christ, as the head of the church, demand submission from the church or does the church submit to the leadership of Christ as a choice?

Read Colossians 3:23-24 V23 How does this verse say we are to do everything in our lives?

Colossians 3:24 Who do we ultimately serve?

Where does the reward for our service to others come from?

Would this also apply to wives that choose to submit to the leadership of their husbands?

Read Titus 3:4 Is the word "saviour" or "savior" listed with a capital when talking about God as our Savior?

Read Titus 3:6 Is the word "saviour" or "savior" listed with a capital when talking about Jesus as our Savior?

Back to Ephesians 5:23 Does the word "saviour" in this verse begin with a capital or not? (in the KJV)

Does this verse refer to the saving of the spirit, soul or body?

Read Romans 8:10 According to this verse what part of man has been saved by Christ?

Read Romans 8:23 What part of man is waiting to be redeemed?

From these verses, can we say that our physical bodies have not been redeemed or saved by Christ our Savior?   Yes or No

In your opinion, would the husband be head over the spiritual, physical or both in the wife's life?

Explain why you chose that answer?

V24 To what is the church subject or submitted?

What examples can you give that would show how the church submits to Christ? You can use examples from your own life and how you submit to Christ because you are part of the church.

In the same way that the church submits to Christ, what practical application relates to husbands and wives?

Is this saying that any woman has to submit to any man as her authority figure or just her own husband?

In what areas are wives to be subject, or submit, to their own husbands?

Does this mean that if your husband asked you to do something that went against the Word, you would have to do it?   Yes   or No

V25 What does Paul instruct husbands to do?
    Allow the wife to shop as often as they want.
    Send flowers weekly to their wife.
    Respect their wives.
    Love their wives.

What comparison does Paul use to show the love husbands should have for their wives?

What was the ultimate example of Christ's love for the church?

***Remember, this lesson is for us, not for our spouses. It is not up to us to expect someone to do something just because we believe they should. Let the Holy Spirit speak to them. He knows how to say things in the right way.

V26 Fill in the blanks: "That he might _____ and _____ it with the _____ of _____ by the _____."

Christ gave himself, out of his love for the church, for a two-fold purpose. Name each below:
1.
2.
Look up each word above, in any source, and write the meaning next to each.

What makes people clean?

What way has Christ established to sanctify and cleanse the church?

What is used as water in this washing of the church?

Read James 1:21-25 Explain what part of you is your soul?

V22 How are we deceived?
    By hearing the Word and thinking on it.
    By doing things that look good to others.
    By hearing the Word and not living it in our lives.

V23-24 What analogy does James give of someone who hears the Word but doesn't live it in their lives?

What does that man forget after he looks in the mirror?

V25 What does James call the Word in this verse?

Look up the word "liberty" in any source and give its meaning:

What does James say is the opposite of being a forgetful hearer?

What result does James give for the one who hears and does the word?

Back to Ephesians 5:26 Does the washing of the Word work to sanctify and cleanse if we don't do it?

What do you or can you do in your own life to be washed with the Word? (Name at least two things)

V27 What is the ultimate purpose Paul gives for Jesus sanctifying and cleansing the church?

What words are used to describe the church?
KJV _____ AOV _____

What two things does AOV say the church will <u>not</u> have because they have been cleansed?
1.
2.

What two things will the church be when they use the Word to be cleansed?
1.
2.

Christ sanctifies and cleanses the church so that he can present her to whom?

Doing the Word: MEMORIZATION

This week, purpose to memorize two scriptures about who you are or what you have because of Christ in you. You can use the In Christ and In Him from Ephesians Chapter One or you may pick your own.

Here are four rules to use in your memorization:
- Personalize the verses by speaking them in the first person. They would be "I" statements. For example, as Paul did with Galatians 2:20 *"I am crucified with Christ, nevertheless I live, yet not I but Christ lives in me and the life that I now live in the flesh I live by the faith of the Son of God who loved me and gave himself for me."*
- (My personal favorite verse.)
- Make them present tense, now statements. "I am" statements.
- Make them positive statements. No negative. This is about our understanding how God sees us not how we see ourselves.
- Begin to picture what it looks like to actually live out the scripture in your life. If it is about the spiritual blessings, how would you be living your life if you walked in every spiritual blessing Jesus purchased for you?

Be prepared to share the overwhelming joy and peace you will feel at the end of your week so that the rest of the class can benefit.

NOTES

SCRIPTURE - WORKSHEET 9
Ephesians 5:29 – 6:9

²⁸ So ought men to love their wives as their own bodies. He that loveth his wife loveth himself.

²⁹ For no man ever yet hated his own flesh; but nourisheth and cherisheth it, even as the Lord the church:

³⁰ for we are members of his body, of his flesh, and of his bones.

³¹ For this cause shall a man leave his father and mother, and shall be joined unto his wife, and they two shall be one flesh.

³² This is a great mystery: but I speak concerning Christ and the church.

³³ Nevertheless let every one of you in particular so love his wife even as himself; and the wife see that she reverence *her* husband.

6 Children, obey your parents in the Lord: for this is right.

² Honour thy father and mother; (which is the first commandment with promise;)

³ that it may be well with thee, and thou mayest live long on the earth.

⁴ And, ye fathers, provoke not your children to wrath: but bring them up in the nurture and admonition of the Lord.

⁵ Servants, be obedient to them that are *your* masters according to the flesh, with fear and trembling, in singleness of your heart, as unto Christ;

⁶ not with eyeservice, as menpleasers; but as the servants of Christ, doing the will of God from the heart;

⁷ with good will doing service, as to the Lord, and not to men:

⁸ knowing that whatsoever good thing any man doeth, the same shall he receive of the Lord, whether *he be* bond or free.

⁹ And, ye masters, do the same things unto them, forbearing threatening: knowing that your Master also is in heaven; neither is there respect of persons with him.

Worksheet 9
Ephesians 5:29 – 6:9
Read Ephesians 5:29 – 6:9 daily and prior to completing this lesson

V28 In the example Paul gives of Christ loving his own body, the church, enough to cleanse her, **(from verses 25-27)** how should husbands love their wives?

Fill in the blanks: "He that _____ his _____ _____ _____."

V29 What is it that no man/person ever hated?

He does two things with his flesh. What are they?
1.
2.
Next to each above, write the description from AOV.

These two actions are an analogy of what?
    How Christ feeds and takes care of the animals.
    How bodies grow.
    How Christ feeds and takes care of the church.

V30 Why does Christ nourish and cherish the church?
    Because the church does everything lovingly.
    Because the church is in unity.
    Because the church is made up of men and women.
    Because the church are members/parts of His body.

What parts of His body does Paul mention?
1.   2.

V31 What does a man leave when being joined in marriage?

What is a man joined to in marriage?

Verse 31 is a quote from **Genesis 2:24**. What word is used there for the phrase "shall be joined unto" in the Ephesians quote?

Look up the word "cleave" in any source and give its meaning:

What do the two become in marriage?

V32 What does Paul say that two becoming one flesh is?

This great mystery of a man and woman becoming one flesh is actually a great mystery of what?

Is this truth that you are a part of Christ's body, the church, a physical feeling or something you know to be true whether you feel it or not?

How do you know that Paul is making a true statement about Christ & the church being one flesh?

V33 In summary, what two principles of marriage does Paul give:
1.
2.

Since we are only responsible for our portion of this verse, give at least two examples of what it looks like to respect or love your spouse?
1.
2.

> DIGGING DEEPER: The words "nourish" and "cherish" used in this verse are related to the raising of children. The Greek meaning of "nourish" is "to rear up to maturity." The Greek meaning of "cherish" is "to brood over" as eggs are protected and cared for by a mother hen. A mother hen will fight off any predator to protect her eggs.
>
> The relationship between a husband and wife is an allegory of Christ and his love and care of the church. Everything being said about the husband is an example of how Christ treats the church, nourishing and cherishing it as it is his body. The body he gave his very life to save.
>
> Wives are told to respect their husbands as the church is to show respect to Christ. Respect is when an important value or esteem is placed on someone which should cause a higher consideration or treatment that is appropriate to that value. We, as the body of Christ, are to place a higher value on Christ than anything or anyone in our lives.
>
> What applies to Christ and the church, applies to husbands and wives. Remember, we are only to do our part as part of the body and with our spouses and not be concerned about theirs. God can take care of the rest of the body and our spouses.

Chapter 6 V1 Who is Paul addressing in this verse?

What does he tell them to do?
    Be sure to ask for expensive things from their parents.
    Be as naughty as possible while growing up.
    Obey their parents in the Lord.

What reason does Paul give for their obedience?

Do children usually want other reasons why they have to obey their parents? Yes or No

What is a child's most asked question when told to do something?

V2 What else does Paul tell children to do?

Paul says this instruction is what?

V3 What are the two aspects of the promise for children who honor their parents in the Lord?
1.

2.

V4 To whom is this verse addressed?

What are they <u>not</u> to do?

What does the word "provoke" mean? (you can use any source)

To what point does Paul tell fathers to <u>NOT</u> provoke their children?

What two things does Paul tell fathers to do to their children? (Write them from each version)
KJV _____ AOV _____
KJV _____ AOV _____

How are all these to be done?

V5 To whom is this verse addressed?

What are they instructed to do?

According to what?

List the two ways in which slaves are instructed to obey their masters:
KJV _____ AOV _____
KJV _____ AOV _____

Epheisans 6:5 (Amplified Version taken from www.biblegateway.com)
"Servants (slaves), be obedient to those who are your physical masters, having respect for them and eager concern to please them, in singleness of motive *and* with all your heart, as [service] to Christ [Himself]."

List the five attitudes from this version, that shows how servants are to obey masters?
1.
2.
3.
4.
5.

V6 What are the two ways in which slaves are <u>not</u> to serve their masters?
KJV _____ AOV _____
KJV _____ AOV _____

In what two ways are slaves to be obedient to their masters?
KJV _____ AOV _____
KJV _____ AOV _____

From whose heart, do you think, they are to do the will of God?

V7 What word does AOV use to describe how servants are to serve their owners?
Fearfully   Reluctantly   Cautiously   Just barely   Within reason   Enthusiastically

As if they were serving who?

As if they were **NOT** serving who?

Could this verse also tell us how we should be in our service to the Lord?
Yes or No
If yes, what way is that?

Look up the word "enthusiasm" in any source and give its meaning:

Could this verse also apply to all relationships in our lives?   Yes or No

*** Part of your lesson for this week is to make a conscious effort to purposefully treat others, in words and actions, as though you were doing it unto the Lord. At the end of this worksheet write what you did or said differently because you know you serve the Lord and not man.

V8 What does Paul assume that the Ephesians know?
- That God meets the need of every human being.
- That God automatically works in a persons life.
- That God rewards those who do what is right in the Lord.

Does it matter what position in life someone holds to receive rewards from the Lord?

Read Colossians 3:23-24.
The reward is part of what?
   Payment due us.   What we have earned.   Our inheritance.

We receive that inheritance because we serve who?

Ephesians 6:9 To whom is this verse addressed?

What are they to stop doing?

What reason does Paul give for them stopping this?

This verse tells masters to treat their slaves "in the same way." What verse combination below best describes what Paul means by this statement:
- Verses 6:1-3
- Verses 6:3-4
- Verses 6:5-7

Verses 5, 6 and 7 describe ways in which believers are to live in a slave/master relationship. Use AOV to describe how Paul relates each to our relationship with Christ and God. These are examples of how we are to treat others with unconditional love.

V5

V6

V7

What does AOV use to describe "neither is there respect of persons with him" from the KJV?

DIGGING DEEPER: The servant-master relationship here can equate to the employee-employer relationship of our day. Paul says that the service we perform to our employer is doing God's will. Notice that Paul makes a distinction between the degree of service to our employer when they are watching and when they are not. If our attitude is to slack off when our employer is not around the bible calls us menpleasers: only doing work to make ourselves look good. Colossians 3:22 says that when we serve as menpleasers we are not showing our reverence for the Lord.

Another point that Paul makes is to serve others with *good will*. Verse 7 says that good will is an attitude determined by our obedience to the Lord and not by whether people deserve it or not. Our attitude in any situation is determined by us. It doesn't matter what personality type or attitude of the other person we are dealing with, we must always do everything as unto the Lord, which is with good will or simple kindness. We know that the kindness that we show to others will make a change in them as they are touched by God's love through us. And Verse 8 says that any good thing that we do, we will receive in return from the Lord. BONUS!!!

What I did and said differently because I know that I serve the Lord and not man:

SPIRITUAL WARFARE WORKSHEETS

NOTES

INTRODUCTION TO SPIRITUAL WARFARE
THE ARMOR

This portion of Ephesians is where Paul explains the power resident in us because of what Jesus Christ has accomplished on our behalf. Also, due to the fact that the Holy Spirit abides in our spirit. Paul compares the completeness of this power to that of a Roman soldier. I believe that Paul uses this example because the Roman soldier was a very powerful presence representing the ruling authority at that time. This was an example that anyone of that time period would understand. However, we don't have Roman soldiers walking around our neighborhood, so the message that would be easily understood by those Paul was immediately addressing with his letter would not be so easily understood by people in the 21st Century.

Therefore, just reading this portion of Paul's letter and not including other aspects that support Paul's analogy of the armor would give us incomplete knowledge of how we can live with the armor intact in our present circumstances. If we can grasp the whole of this powerful portion of scripture related to who we are in Christ, it will give us a clearer understanding of what the real battle is and the position we already possess because of what Christ has accomplished.

The next four worksheets explain the armor of God as it is used in spiritual warfare. This section of study will answer the questions:
- Where is the battle fought?
- What is the battle over?
- How do I use the armor?
- What does putting on the armor really mean?
- How does the armor relate to the rest of the letter to the Ephesians?

A Bible is necessary in this section to answer a good portion of the questions. Not all scripture references are included.

SPIRITUAL WARFARE: This section of the Ephesians study can be used as a stand-alone study on Spiritual Warfare.

SCRIPTURE - SPIRITUAL WARFARE
WORKSHEET 1

Psalm 8 KJV

1 O Lord, our Lord, how excellent is Thy name in all the earth, who hast set Thy glory above the heavens!
2 Out of the mouth of babes and sucklings hast Thou ordained strength because of Thine enemies, that Thou mightest still the enemy and the avenger.
3 When I consider Thy heavens, the work of Thy fingers, the moon and the stars which Thou hast ordained,
4 what is man that Thou art mindful of him, and the son of man that Thou dost visit him?
5 For Thou hast made him a little lower than the angels, and hast crowned him with glory and honor.
6 Thou hast made him to have dominion over the works of Thy hands; Thou hast put all things under his feet,
7 all sheep and oxen, yea, and the beasts of the field,
8 the fowl of the air, and the fish of the sea, and whatsoever passeth through the paths of the seas.
9 O Lord, our Lord, how excellent is Thy name in all the earth!

Spiritual Warfare – Worksheet 1

<u>Who is Man and what did God give him.</u> **Read Psalm 8**
Psalm 8:1 To whom is this Psalm talking?

V4 Who is being talked about in this verse? (pick one)
                    Animals, God, Man, Plants.

What is the first portion of this question that is asked of God regarding man?
(fill in) "What is _____ that _____ art _____ of him."

According to that portion of this question, what is God doing toward man?

Who is the second portion of this question talking about? (pick one)
                    Animals, God, Plants, the son of man.

What is the second thing that God does regarding the son of man?
KJV _____ AOV _____

V5 What is the first thing the writer says about this man that God has created?
KJV
AOV

What is the second thing the writer says about this man that God has created?
KJV
AOV

V6 What is the first thing the writer says about God's assignment of man in this verse?
KJV
AOV

What is the second thing the writer says about God's assignment of man in this verse?
KJV
AOV

What does man have dominion over?

What is put under man's feet?

Who gave man dominion and put all things under his feet?

Read Genesis 1:28 List below the things that man has dominion over?

What happened to man at the fall?
Read Genesis 3:17-19 This is where God tells Adam the consequences for eating of the Tree of the knowledge of Good and Evil.

Does this say that God took Adam's dominion away?
    Yes or No

There are two things that God did say would happen to Adam from V17 and V19. List them:
V17

V19

What is it that man <u>still has</u> over the works of God's hands from Psalm 8:6 even though man will have to work harder than he would have since he ate of the tree that God said "Do not eat of this tree"?

What does that mean to you to know that mankind still has dominion over the works of God's hands?

Sin entered and what Jesus did.
Read Romans 5:12-19 V12 What entered the world by what Adam did?

What came upon man because of sin?

Was death passed upon *all* men ever to be born on earth because of Adam's sin?   Yes or No

V18 By one man's offense or deviation from truth what came upon all men?

By the righteous act of one man (Jesus) what was the result for all men?

Even though we were not physically with Adam eating the apple, were we still born into the same sin that Adam committed?   Yes or No

V19 Even though we were not physically with Jesus in his death, burial and resurrection, are we still able to partake of what Jesus accomplished, making us righteous?   Yes or No

Who is satan?
Read Ezekiel 28:12-19 This describes who satan was and what happened at his fall.
V14 What does this verse say that satan was?

What is a cherub?   Man, God, Angel, Demon.

Read Hebrews 1:13-14 V13 Who is being talked about in these verses?

V14 What does this verse say that angels are?
   1. Cute little cupids with bows.   2. Ghosts.   3. Ministering spirits.

To whom are angels to minister?

At the very best that satan could have been, what would he have been doing in his relationship to man?

Does this say that satan is all powerful?   Yes or No

Does this say that satan is equal to God, in any way?   Yes or No

Does this say that satan is equal to man, in any way?   Yes or No

<u>Who has authority?</u>
Read Colossians 2:12-15
V12 What two things happen to us at the same time that something was happening to Jesus?
(Look for the verbs prior to each statement "with Him")
1.   2.

V14 What was blotted out on our behalf by what Jesus had done?

V15 What did Jesus spoil or disarm?
1.   2.

What did he make of them?

How did he make them a public display?

What does it mean to triumph over something or someone?

According to these verses, did Jesus totally defeat satan, principalities and powers?   Yes or No

According to these verses, should satan be a problem for the believer?
Yes or No

<u>How to handle the devil?</u>
Read James 4:5-8
V5 God's desire is to connect with us through whom that lives within us?

V6 What is it that God gives?

To whom does he give grace?

V7 In order to have this relationship with God through the Spirit and receive more grace, what is the first thing this verse tells us to do?

What does this verse tell us to do in relationship to the devil?

What does this verse say will be the result when we resist the devil?

Which meaning from the Webster's dictionary for the word "resist" best describes how we resist the devil in light of Jesus' complete and total victory over the devil, as we submit ourselves to God: (pick one)
- To fight against, to try to stop or prevent.
- To remain strong against the force of, to not be affected or harmed by.
- To prevent yourself from doing something that you want to do.

Who is responsible to submit to God and resist the devil?

List some ways that you submit yourself to God:

List some ways that you resist the devil:

<u>Where is the power now?</u>
Read Matthew 28:18 Who is speaking in this verse?

What was given to Jesus?

In what areas does this power work?

According to this verse, who has the power and authority now?

Continue on the next page to Recap what you have just learned.

Recap Spiritual Warfare Worksheet 1:

Who still has dominion or rule over the work of God's hands now?

Has satan been defeated?

Who made an open show of defeat of satan?

Is satan a problem for the believer?

At the very best that satan could have been, what would he had been doing in relationship to man or human beings?

How does the believer handle satan?

Who has the authority according to Matthew 28:18?

NOTES

SCRIPTURE - SPIRITUAL WARFARE
WORKSHEET 2

2 Corinthians 10:1-5   KJV
1 Now I Paul myself beseech you by the meekness and gentleness of Christ, who in presence am base among you, but being absent am bold toward you:
2 But I beseech you, that I may not be bold when I am present with that confidence, wherewith I think to be bold against some, which think of us as if we walked according to the flesh.
3 For though we walk in the flesh, we do not war after the flesh:
4 (For the weapons of our warfare are not carnal, but mighty through God to the pulling down of strong holds;)
5 Casting down imaginations, and every high thing that exalteth itself against the knowledge of God, and bringing into captivity every thought to the obedience of Christ;

Romans 8   KJV
5 For those who are according to the flesh mind the things of the flesh; but those who are according to the Spirit, the things of the Spirit.
6 For to be carnally minded is death, but to be spiritually minded is life and peace,
7 because the carnal mind is enmity against God, for it is not subject to the law of God, neither indeed can be.
8 So then, those who are in the flesh cannot please God.

Spiritual Warfare – Worksheet 2
Review Recap from Spiritual Warfare Worksheet 1 then continue.

<u>Covenant of Promise</u>.
Read Galatians 3:14-16
V16 Who is this verse talking about?
    Jesus and God.
    Satan and Jesus.
    Abraham and his Seed.

What was made to Abraham and his Seed?

Paul wants to make it clear that the promises were not made to whom?

He explains that "And to seeds" would mean what?
    As of plants.
    As of weeds.
    As of many.

V14 To whom is the <u>seed</u> that Paul says the promises of God were made?

Who resides in the believer?

Are we correct in saying that the promises of God were made to Jesus and Jesus has all power and authority? Yes or No

Would Jesus believe that His authority and power work over anything opposing God's will? Yes or No

Would Jesus completely trust what God has said regarding the promises working in a believer's life? Yes or No

<u>Where is the battle?</u>
Read 2 Corinthians 10:1-5 KJV
V1 What attitude did Paul say he was going to have because he was absent from them?

V2 There is a boldness that Paul speaks about that he uses against others that think what of Paul and the Corinthians?
   That they don't volunteer enough.
   That they walk in fear.
   That they walk according to the flesh.
   That they like the cookies and linger in the foyer.

Write below the description for "acting according to the flesh" from AOV.

What do you think "walk according to the flesh" looks like in someone's life?

V3 How does Paul say that he and the Corinthians live?

What is it that Paul says we do <u>not</u> do after the flesh? (pick one)
   Speak, Sing, Run, Jump, War, Play, Worship.

Can we say from these verses that the war that a believer fights is not done on a fleshly or worldly level using weapons that are used in human combat?
   Yes or No

***The weapons that a believer uses will be discussed in Spiritual Warfare Worksheet 3 & 4. For now it is beneficial that we understand that we don't war against human beings using human weapons.

V4 How does Paul describe what our weapons are <u>not</u>?
KJV _____ AOV _____

What word is used to describe the types of weapons we have?

What do these weapons destroy?

What words are used to describe what the weapons do to strongholds?
KJV _____ AOV _____

V5 What is the first thing that is destroyed by our weapons?   KJV

What is done to this first thing?
KJV _____   AOV _____

There are other words used to describe "imaginations." Look up the words below in any source and give their meanings:
Arguments

Theories

Reasonings

Is Paul saying that strongholds are wrong thoughts that we allow to come into our minds?   Yes or No

What is the next thing listed that is destroyed by our weapons?

What words does AOV use for those "high things"?
1.   2.

What do imaginations and high things try to do?

What is the last thing listed in this verse, that is destroyed by our weapons?

What are we to do with every thought?
    Bring it to the pastor.
    Bring it to someone who cares.
    Bring it into captivity.

To what is that thought brought into captivity?

From these verses, is Paul saying that it is possible for us to cast down imaginations and capture thoughts that are not obedient to Christ and bring them into obedience to Christ?   Yes or No

If No, explain why:

If Yes, what do believers have that can capture thoughts and imaginations? (V4)

What percentage of the time do you think that Paul thought the weapons he speaks of will work against thoughts, imaginations and high things?
  25% of the time.   50% of the time.   75% of the time.   All the time.

The weapons that these verses are talking about work against what?
    Anyone I am having trouble with at the time.
    To fight every demon in hell.
    Thoughts, imaginations and high things that are contrary to God.

<u>How deep are our thoughts?</u>
1 Chronicles 28:9
With what two things does David tell Solomon to serve God?
1.
2.

What two things does David say about what the Lord does in regard to the heart and mind?
1.
2.

If you seek God, will you be able to find or have a relationship with him?
    Yes or No
Does God know what is going on in your heart and mind?
    Yes or No

What would a willing mind that serves God be thinking?

Genesis 6:5
What was in man just prior to the flood?

What was the level of this wickedness?
                Small, medium or great. (pick one)

Complete this portion of **verse 5** from the KJV or NKJV:
"and that _____ _____ of the _____
of his _____ were _____ _____ _____."

Where were these imaginations in these people?

What was the content of these imaginations?

How often were these evil imaginations in the thoughts of the heart of these people?

Can we say from this verse that thoughts don't just stay in our minds but go down to the deepest part of us, our heart?   Yes or No

Proverbs 4:23 What is it that comes out of the heart?

<u>What is the fight?</u>
Read Romans 8:5-8 (included)
V5 What does this verse say that those who live according to the flesh do?
 KJV

AOV

V6 What other phrase is used here that was the word *flesh* in verse 5?

What happens to those who are carnally minded?

Are carnally minded people dropping like flies all around us? Yes or No

If no, then does this verse mean a different kind of death than leaving this earth? Yes or No

Which one of the following would best describe the death carnally minded people experience:
    The permanent end of life.
     Not being able to enjoy the benefits of a life lived with a loving Father.

What is the opposite of being carnally minded?

What are the results for those who choose to live their lives by the leading of the Holy Spirit?

V7 What two reasons does Paul give for the carnal mind leading to death? KJV
1.
2.

Write these same answers from AOV.
1.
2.

V8 What kind of a relationship do fleshly/carnal/self-centered people have with God?

What is it that causes people to live without life and peace? (v6)

What would you think would be examples of living fleshly minded?

1 Timothy 6:12
What type of a fight does Paul tell Timothy to fight?

What do you think faith is?

What do you have to fight for in a fight of faith?

From this Worksheet, what have you learned about where the believer's battle is fought?

What are two areas of thought in your own life that need to be brought to the obedience of Christ?

1.

2.

One of the weapons that we will be learning about is the Sword of the Spirit which is the word of God. Take some time to look up a verse or verses that would cast down or take captive these wrong thoughts from each answer above. List them below, personalize them and proclaim them everyday.

1.

2.

Recap Spiritual Warfare Worksheet 2:
To whom was the covenant of promise made?
   Man, Woman, Angels, Jesus.
What do our weapons pull down or overthrow and destroy?

What are these strongholds?

What are these thoughts and imaginations against?

What would our faith be in that strongholds would be trying to hold strong?

SCRIPTURE - SPIRITUAL WARFARE
WORKSHEET 3

Ephesians 6:10-15

[10] Finally, my brethren, be strong in the Lord, and in the power of his might.

[11] Put on the whole armour of God, that ye may be able to stand against the wiles of the devil.

[12] For we wrestle not against flesh and blood, but against principalities, against powers, against the rulers of the darkness of this world, against spiritual wickedness in high *places*.

[13] Wherefore take unto you the whole armour of God, that ye may be able to withstand in the evil day, and having done all, to stand.

[14] Stand therefore, having your loins girt about with truth, and having on the breastplate of righteousness;

[15] and your feet shod with the preparation of the gospel of peace;

Spiritual Warfare – Worksheet 3
Review Recap from Spiritual Warfare Worksheet 2 then continue.

Read Ephesians 6:10-11

V10 What is the first word Paul uses to begin this section of his letter?

> DIGGING DEEPER: The word "finally" is more important than just a word describing the end of Paul's thoughts. Rick Renner in his book *"Dressed to Kill"* describes the extreme importance contained in the word "finally." *"In conclusion, I have saved the most important issue of this epistle until the end. That way if you remember nothing else of what I have said, you will remember this. I want this to stand out in your mind!"* (Rick Renner, Dressed to Kill [Harrison House Publishers, © 1991]pg. 143)

To whom is this addressed?

What two things does Paul tell these believers?
1.
2.

Is the believer told to be strong in his own might? Yes or No

If not, then whose?

From the last question on Spiritual Warfare Worksheet 1, who has the power and authority now?

V11 Whose armor is Paul talking about in this verse? God or Man.

What are we to do with God's armor?

What will God's armor help us to do?

What does AOV use for the word "wiles"?

According to **Colossians 2:12-15** Is satan a defeated foe? Yes or No

Read 2 Corinthians 4:4
What does satan do to get people to be tricked into walking in unbelief?

He would be blinding their eyes to what to get them to walk in unbelief?

Ephesians 6:12 What is it that we do not wrestle against?

Who would be "flesh and blood"?

Paul says our fight is against what four entities?
1.
2.
3.
4.

From Spiritual Warfare Worksheet 2 where did we conclude that the battle was fought?   On the earth, In the heavenlies, At your house, In the mind.

> DIGGING DEEPER: Has Jesus overcome principalities, powers, mights and dominions?   Yes or No?   Yes!
> So then, we don't fight demons in the atmosphere, we fight the influence in our minds. The fight is against contrary thoughts that go against the truths of God.

V13 What statement from **V11** is the same as what we are told to, "*take unto you,*" in this verse?

What does Paul want us to be able to do while we have on the armor?

Read Ephesians 5:16
In what kind of days were the Ephesians living?

Have those days ended? Yes or No   If yes, tell me when?

Ephesians 6:13 Paul is telling us to stand after doing what?

In your opinion, what do you think the statement "having done all" means?

> DIGGING DEEPER: At no point in the fight do we give up or stop depending on our armor to accomplish. We must remember that the struggle the Ephesians were going through was in the most disgusting, vile, evil atmosphere on the earth at that time. Paul had to address their commitment to stay strong so the Ephesians would not fall back into what was familiar or comfortable and going on all around them, even though it was wrong. Part of our struggle with this new life is not to go back into what was comfortable.

V14 What are the first two words at the beginning of this verse?

Look up the word "stand" in any source and find the meaning that would apply here?

What is worn as a belt or on our loins?

John 1:14-17
What was the Word made so that the Word could dwell among us?

That Word was full of what two things?
1.   2.

According to **verse 17** grace and truth are in whom?

John 8:31-32
V32 What is it that this verse says we will know?

Knowing that truth will do what?

According to **verse 31** how do we get the knowledge of this truth?

Write below two things you do in your own life to continue in the word.
1.
2.

Is there a difference between just knowing of the Word and having an experienced knowledge of the Word?   Yes or No

Which one of the above types of knowing do you think will stand in the evil days?

In your opinion, what does experienced knowledge of the Word look like in your own life?

In Ephesians 6:14
What type of a breastplate is a part of the armor?

2 Corinthians 5:21
Who was made sin?

Who was it that made Jesus sin? (v20 might help)

Jesus was made sin for whom?

Did Jesus ever experience sin? Yes or No

Explain your answer:

Who is the "we" in this verse?

What were the "we" made?

Who is the "him" in this verse?

What was the purpose in Jesus being made sin?

What part do you play in being made righteous?

With righteousness as a part of the armor, do you already possess it or need to get it?

How do you or did you get righteousness?

Ephesians 4:21-24
V22 What are we to do with that old man?

Paul says that our old man was our former way of life. Even though I might have considered myself a good person before I made Jesus my Lord and Savior, what type of a worldly atmosphere was my influence?
> Where everything was perfect.
> Where nothing ever went wrong and everyone loved me.
> A sinful atmosphere where satan worked to corrupt mankind.

Would my old man decisions have been made by a godly or sinful influence?

What 2 things can change the former way of life I lived that was influenced by a sinful atmosphere?
V22
V24

What are two aspects of how that new man was created?
1.
2.

DIGGING DEEPER: I have learned a get application from Dr. Jim Richards regarding putting off and putting on. How do we put off those contrary thoughts that are influenced by that dead old man? Sit quietly and focused and send it away. I say "I send you away. I am not that person. That thing is no longer an influence in my life." It really is that simple.

You put on by speaking the truth of the Word of God that contradicts that contrary thought. Picture it completed in your mind by pondering on it so that you can get it down into your heart. For sickness put on Isaiah 53:5.

Ephesians 5:9
Would "the children of light" be part of the new man from Ephesians 4:24?

What are the three fruits of the Spirit that the new man or children of light have? 1.   2.   3.

2 Timothy 3:16-17
V16 What is the subject of this verse?
                God, Jesus, devil, scripture, inspiration.

Scripture is profitable for what four things?
1.
2.
3.
4.

V17 According to this verse, what benefit does the man of God get from scripture?
    Able to leap tall buildings in a single bound.
    It will make him complete.
    Makes man strong beyond his years.
    Thoroughly furnished unto every good work.

Why would you think believers need instruction in righteousness if the new man that we are because of Jesus in us was already made righteous?

What have you learned about righteousness?
(notate each with T for true, F for false)
  I am righteous because of what I do.
  I was made righteous because of what Jesus Christ has done.
  I must accept that I am righteous by faith.
  My old man is righteous.
  I need to put off the old man and his sin influenced ways.
  My new man was created righteous and holy.
  I am really the new man, not the old man.
  My old man cannot be changed, it's dead.
  I can become more righteous by doing the Word.
  Scripture shows me how to live out of my spirit or my new man.
  Scripture shows me how I was made righteous.
  To walk out righteousness in my life, I must believe that I am righteous.

Ephesians 6:15 What kind of shoes are on our feet?

Is there more than one type of gospel? Yes or No

Read Romans 10:15 and Isaiah 52:7 Romans 10:15 is a quote from Isaiah 52:7.

From Romans 10:15 Complete this statement from the KJV:
How beautiful are the feet of those who...
1.
2.

From Isaiah 52:7 Complete this statement from the KJV:
How beautiful upon the mountains are the feet of him that...
1.
2.
3.
4.
5.

Are good news, peace, glad tidings and salvation all talking about what Jesus brought to us?
    Yes or No

Read 2 Corinthians 5:17-21
V17 What does this verse say we are in Christ?

V18 As we live in this new man, are all things of the old man or of God?

How are we reconciled to God?

What ministry have we been given because we are this new man?

What do you think "reconciliation" means?

V19 What are the three aspects of what God, being in Christ has done for believers?
1.
2.
3

V20 What does Paul call himself and Timothy in this verse?

Look up the word "ambassador" and give its meaning:

Do these verses describe someone who already has the "gospel of peace"?

Back to Ephesians 6:15
What word does the KJV use that would be the same as "ready to preach" when talking about the gospel?

What does it mean to you to be prepared to preach the gospel of peace?

In your own words, what is the gospel of peace?

Recap Spiritual Warfare Worksheet 3
What is the first word that Paul uses in the beginning of his talk about the armor?

How much of the armor are we to wear?

Where is the battle that is against principalities, powers, rulers and spiritual wickedness?

What is the first piece of armor that Paul describes as a belt?

Where do we find the truth?

What is the second piece of armor that Paul describes as a breastplate?

Do we work toward righteousness or are we made righteous by what Jesus Christ has done?

What is the third piece of armor that Paul describes as shoes?

Breifly explain what the gospel of peace is:

NOTES

SCRIPTURE - SPIRITUAL WARFARE
WORKSHEET 4

Ephesians 6:16-21

¹⁶ above all, taking the shield of faith, wherewith ye shall be able to quench all the fiery darts of the wicked.

¹⁷ And take the helmet of salvation, and the sword of the Spirit, which is the word of God:

¹⁸ praying always with all prayer and supplication in the Spirit, and watching thereunto with all perseverance and supplication for all saints;

¹⁹ and for me, that utterance may be given unto me, that I may open my mouth boldly, to make known the mystery of the gospel,

²⁰ for which I am an ambassador in bonds: that therein I may speak boldly, as I ought to speak.

²¹ But that ye also may know my affairs, *and* how I do, Tychicus, a beloved brother and faithful minister in the Lord, shall make known to you all things:

Spiritual Warfare Worksheet 4
Review the Recap from Spiritual Warfare Worksheet 3 then continue.

Ephesians 6:16 What are the first two words in this verse from the KJV?

What is a believers shield?

What can you do with faith?

What does AOV call the fiery darts?

At what are the darts shot?

> DIGGING DEEPER: Why does Paul say "Above all" regarding faith and not for the other parts of the armor: salvation, the gospel of peace, the Word of God, righteousness? If we did not have faith to believe that we have obtained theother parts of the armor by what Jesus Christ has done, we would not be able to stand against <u>any</u> attack. Faith is the key! It is how it all works. It is how we enter into the Kingdom of God. The most important thing we can do in our new life with Christ is do whatever it takes to live by faith in the finished work of Christ.

Hebrews 11:1 Faith consists of two aspects. List them below:
1.
2.

Is this verse saying that faith is "confidence for things that are not seen but hoped for"?
    Yes or No

Hebrews 11 is the Hall of Fame of those who lived by faith. Does the same description of faith "confidence for things that are not seen but hoped for" apply in their lives as well as ours?
    Yes or No

In the lives of those Old Testament men and women of faith, were the things they did not see but hoped for:
    Things that they had decided they wanted.
    Things that God had told them they would receive.

Hebrews 8:6 What kind of a covenant did Jesus obtain for believers after his death, burial and resurrection?

What are the benefits of this better covenant?

Would these better promises be things that we use <u>faith for</u> to reach out and receive from God?

2 Peter 1:1 To whom is Peter talking?

How did they obtain that faith?

According to this verse, is faith:
    Something you have to build up in yourself to receive things from God.
    Received because of God's righteous plan through Jesus Christ.

Philemon 6 How does our faith stay effective or active?

From what you've learned so far, name two things that are in Christ Jesus?
1.
2.

Now acknowledge by your confession that those same things are in you!!

DIGGING DEEPER: Looking at the Greek meaning of the words in Hebrews 11:1 describing faith, it would be better to say that "Faith is assurance and proof of desires expected to be obtained." These are not just any desires that we want. Thank the Lord for that! Sometimes our selfish desires can come up with some amazing things. We have better promises to live out that Jesus has already obtained through his death, burial and resurrection. Promises thoroughly thought out by God to be the perfect fulfillment of his total plan for man. Having a intimate personal knowledge of the Better Covenant that Jesus obtained for us is where faith begins.

Ephesians 6:17 What is the piece of armor mentioned first in this verse?

What needs to be covered by a helmet, that needs protecting regarding your salvation?
    1. Hair   2. Makeup   3. Skull   4. Mind

What does the mind do? (Pick all that apply)
    It thinks and reasons and drives decisions.
    It receives information from the five senses.
    It is the doorway to the heart.

Ephesians 1:13 What did the Ephesians hear that caused them to trust in Christ?

What else does Paul call the Word of Tuth?

What did the Ephesians have to do, after they heard the truth of the gospel, to receive salvation and be sealed with the Holy Spirit?
    Think good thoughts in their minds.
    Become really holy to receive.
    Trust and believe in Christ and what he had accomplished.

In your own words, explain what you believe salvation to be?

What would be the benefit of having salvation as a helmet?

> DIGGING DEEPER: The word "salvation" is the root word *soteria*. It consists of restoration of right relationship and the original intent of God for man, preservation or keeping in good condition, health, soundness and deliverance. Specifically, deliverance is described in more detail as "deliverance from the molestation of enemies." We know the bible says that our enemies are not flesh and blood, and that our enemies set up strongholds in our minds, if we allow them. Therefore, we fight these enemy attacks in our minds by countering them with truths of salvation, restoration, health, deliverance, preservation, and soundness.

Ephesians 6:17 What is the next piece of armor listed in this verse?

What is the sword of the Spirit?

Isaiah 55:11-12 V11 Is this verse talking about the words that God speaks out of His mouth?

Would the words God speaks be the Bible? Yes or No

Which of the following best describes what happens to God's words after he speaks them?
    1. They disappear.   2. They mean nothing.   3. They return to him.

There are two ways that God's Words return to him. Write them below:
1.

2.

V12 What are the two benefits for those who live God's Word as a lifestyle?
1.

2.

Hebrews 4:12
What three words are used here to describe the Word of God?
1.
2.
3.

Write next to 1 & 2 above, the words used for each from AOV of the Bible.

What weaponry does the writer of Hebrews compare to the Word of God?

From the KJV statement below, write the same statement from AOV below:
    "piercing even to the dividing asunder"
_____

What does this two-edged sword divide or separate?
_____ from the _____
_____ from the _____

What word does AOV use for the KJV word "discerner"?

What is the two-edged sword able to discern or judge?

> DIGGING DEEPER: Our sword is the Word of God. There are 2 Greek definitions for "word." *Logos* and *Rhema*. Logos is more than just the written Word. It is the integrity that comes with that Word, which is based on the integrity of God. *Rhema* is the spoken word that has a definite meaning. It's almost like it is speaking directly to you alone. *(The only way to get a Rhema word from God is to be in the Word.)* The sword that Paul is talking about is not like the long pointed sword in the movies. The Roman soldiers sword was about 19 inches long with a curled up tip. Its purpose was to kill and not just wound the enemy. When used, the soldier would stab, twist and remove, taking the insides that were attached to the curled up end. This is the completeness of the Word of God. Not only does it immobilize the thought or imagination, but when used properly, it removes anything that could remain that would cause that thing to be revitalized.

Psalm 89:34 If God makes a covenant with anyone will he ever break or cancel that covenant?   Yes or No

If something is spoken out of God's mouth does he ever change what he has said?   Yes or No

2 Corinthians 1:19-20 V19 From this verse where would you find the promises of God?

V20 There are two things that the promises of God are to the believer. What are they?
1.   2.

How many of God's promises is this verse talking about?

What benefit is there for God to have all his promises to man through Christ be Yes (confirmed) and Amen (accessible)?

In your own life, how would this happen?

Ephesians 6:18 What is the subject of this verse?   Tithe,   Grace,   Prayer.

How often are we to pray?

Who aids us in our prayers? Our friends, The pastor, The Spirit.

We are to watch with perseverance and supplication for all saints. What word does AOV use for the word "watch"?

1 John 5:13-15 V13 Who is John expecting to read this letter?

V14 What is it that believers should have in God?

What is our confidence to be in?
> If we ask, we know he hears.
> If we know his will, we know he hears.
> If we ask according to his will, we know he hears.

Who would be the perfect example of someone who fulfilled God's will?

V15 Because we know that he hears us when we ask according to his will, what is the result?

Does this mean that we should expect God's Word to accomplish what it is sent to accomplish?   Yes or No

Would Isaiah 55, Hebrews 4, Psalm 89 and 2 Corinthians 1, from the study of the Sword as the Word, be saying that we could take God's promises, apply them to our lives by believing and speaking them, then we can expect God's Word to accomplish what it is supposed to accomplish because we know he hears us?   Yes or No

Take one area where you need to stand on a promise of God, find that promise in the Word and write it below. Ask God to fulfill his promise in your life. If we know that he hears us, then we should be thanking him in anticipation every time we think of that promise.

Ephesians 6:19
V19 Paul asks the Ephesians to pray that the message he speaks will confidently make what known?

V20 How does Paul speak of himself?

Paul wants prayer for confidence to do what?

V21 What two things does Paul say about Tychicus?
1.
2.

What can Tychicus tell the Ephesians about Paul?

V22 What reason does Paul give for sending Tychicus?

V23 Paul is talking about whom in this verse?

What two things does Paul want them to have?

Who are the two people that peace and love with faith come from?
1.
2.

V24 Write out Paul's closing statement below.
_____
_____
_____
_____

What is it that Paul desires for the Ephesians to have?

Recap Spiritual Warfare
Who still has dominion or rule over the work of God's hands now?

Has satan been defeated?

Who made an open show of defeat of satan?

Is satan a problem for the believer?

At the very best that satan could have been, what would he had been doing in relationship to man?

How does the believer handle satan?

To whom was the covenant of promise made?
   Man,   Woman,   Angels,   Jesus.
What do our weapons pull down or overthrow and destroy?

What are these strongholds?

What are these thoughts and imaginations against?

What would our faith be in that strongholds would be trying to hold strong?

How much of the armor are we to wear?

Where is the battle that is against principalities, powers, rulers and spiritual wickedness?

Do you have your armor on all the time?

Is there any reason to ever take it off?

Write below those things that stood out to you, changed your thinking or affected your life from the study of Ephesians: (Writing things out is another way to help your mind and heart retain information and grow.)

I have heard some believers say that they get up every morning and put on the armor by speaking each piece over their body. The only reason to do that is if you took it off which from this study we have learned that we have the armor on all the time. Each piece of armor represents what we already have because we are IN CHRIST.

Not being moved from who you are in Christ is ARMOR!

I pray that your life has changed, your relationship with your loving heavenly Father has deepened and your understanding of who God has created you to be "in Christ" has been enlightened because of doing this study.

We all are striving for the same goal.
In Christ,
Sonie

ANSWER KEY SECTION

NOTES

Worksheet 1 Ephesians 1:1 – 1:16   Answer Key

V1 Who is the author of this letter?
Paul.
What does Paul call himself in this letter?
Apostle.
How was Paul given this position?
By the will of God.
To what two groups is this letter written?
Saints in Ephesus.
Faithful in Christ Jesus.

V2 What two things does Paul want the Ephesians to have?
Grace.
Peace.
From where do these two things come?
God our Father.
The Lord Jesus Christ.

2 Peter 1:2 How does Peter say that grace and peace can be increased in our lives?
Through the Knowledge of God.

Ephesians 1:3 Who are the first two people who are blessed?
God the Father.
The Lord Jesus Christ.
Who is the "us" that receives blessings from these two people?
Believers.
Look up the word "blessed" in any source and give its meaning below:
*** See Digging Deeper.
What is the blessing that the "us" receives?
Spiritual Blessings.
Where are they from?
Heavenly places.
In whom are they?
Christ.
If they are in Christ, try to name every place that Christ is, at this very moment?
In the believer by the Holy Spirit, seated at the right hand of God.

In your opinion, what would you think spiritual blessings would be?
All the benefits of heaven-perfect health, wholeness, every need supplied, life lived as if my father were the King of the Universe as I live on earth.

V4 Name who the following people are that are spoken about in this verse?
He _____God_____
Him _____Jesus_____ (only the 1ˢᵗ one mentioned)

What did "he" do?
  Chose us.
When did that last answer take place?
  Before the foundation of the World.
Who is the "we" in this verse? (V1 will help answer this)
  Saints and faithful in Christ Jesus.
What two things are listed as what we have been chosen to be?
  Holy.   *Blameless.*

V5 Look up the word "predestine" in any source?
  *** *See Digging Deeper.*
To what does this verse say we have been predestined?
  Adoption of children.
Through whom did this happen?
  Jesus Christ.
Why did this happen?
  According to the good pleasure of His will.
Explain what you think "to the good pleasure of his will" means?
  The Greek implies the delight of what God determines shall be done.
What is the reason God choose to adopt us as his children through Jesus?
  Because of His love.

V6 Write out verse 6 from AOV of the bible:
_____
_____
According to verses 5 and 6, what 2 reasons are given for God to adopt us as children?
    Because he was in a good mood that day.
    Because of his goodwill and plan.   ****yes
    Because Jesus had nothing to do.
    To bring honor/praise to his glorious grace.   ****yes
According to V6, what did God do that enabled us to be included in the beloved?
    Made us accepted.
What was this adoption?   As servants   As slaves   As friends   <u>As children.</u>

V7 How were we redeemed?
    Through Christ's blood.
What comes to us because of this redemption?
    Forgiveness of sins.

Complete the following from verse 7: We receive forgiveness for our failures/sins because of : _____The riches of His grace._____

In your own words, explain what "grace" is?
   ***See Digging Deeper.*

V8 What verb(s) is used to describe how God gave us this grace?
KJV _____*abounded.*_____ AOV _____

How was this done? Circle all that apply:
   "with judgment, evil, *wisdom*, suffering, good works, *understanding*."
Do you <u>feel</u> like you abound with wisdom and understanding? Yes or <u>No</u>

Do you still have wisdom and understanding? <u>Yes</u> or No

How do you know that you have wisdom and understanding?
   Because the Bible tells me so!!!

V9 What has been made known unto us?
KJV ___*Mystery of his will.*___ AOV _____

This was made known according to what?
   His good pleasure.
Complete the following from the verses below:
God's goodwill and plan or the good pleasure of His will was to do what 2 things?
V5 *Adopt us as children.*
V9 *Make known to us the mystery of His will.*

This mystery was intended to be accomplished through whom?
KJV _____*Himself*_____ AOV _____

V10 What time frame is this verse talking about?
KJV ___*Dispensation of the fullness of times.*_____
AOV _____

What will happen?
   To bring all things together in Christ.
All things will be gathered together from what 2 places?
   Things in heaven.   *Things in earth.*
Who will these things be gathered together in?
   In Christ.
V11 What else has been obtained?
   An inheritance.

Through whom?
Christ.
By what were we predestined?
According to the purpose of God.
Complete the following according to this verse:
"God accomplishes everything........"
    According to what's going on in the world.
    According to how we feel.
    According to what mankind says.
    According to His own design and will. ****yes

V12 Fill in the blanks from the KJV: "That __we__ should be to the __praise__ of _His_ __glory__ who first ____trusted____ in ____Christ____."

Look up the following word in any source and give their meaning:
Praise: Greek: "commendation, to be a praise to a person or thing."
Glory: Greek: "of the majesty of His saving grace."

What were those who first put their trust in Christ made to be?
To the praise of his glory.
In your opinion, describe what is "God's glory"?
God's manifested presence in visible form through healing, prosperity and touching people's lives with goodness.
In your own life, how do you think you bring praise to God's glory?
By loving actions that touch people with his healing power and ministering. Truth to them. Keeping my thoughts full of the Word and casting out anything that is not truth.

V13 In whom did the Ephesians trust? (V12)
Christ.
What did they have to hear before they trusted in Christ?
The Word of truth.
The KJV describes what they heard as what?
The gospel of their salvation.
From your own life, how would you explain to someone what the "gospel of your salvation" is?
The truth about God's love and the extent to which God went, through what Jesus Christ has done, to get man back into a relationship and release man from bondage.

After they heard the "Word of truth," what did they do?
They believed.
What did they receive?
The Holy Spirit.

What verb is used to describe what happened when they received the Holy Spirit?
   Sealed. *****See Digging Deeper.**

V14 From the KJV what is the Holy Spirit?
   The earnest of our inheritance.
What word does AOV use for "earnest"?
   Down payment.

Until what happens?	Of what?
The redemption.	*The purchased possession.*

V15 What was it that Paul heard about the Ephesians? (pick all that apply)
   That they were complaining about the coffee served at church.
   That their evangelism numbers were increasing.
   Of their faith in the Lord Jesus.   ******yes**
   Of their love for God's people.   ******yes**

V16 What two things did Paul do because of what he had heard about the Ephesians?
   Didn't stop giving thanks for the Ephesians.
   Always mentioned them in his prayers.

The words **in Christ, in him,** and **in whom** are listed nine times in Ephesians 1:1-16. Read through this portion of scripture and highlight them on your KJV scripture sheet.

Write in the notes section or on a separate sheet of paper what each scripture is saying in relation to the statements **in Christ, in him or in whom**.

NOTES

Worksheet 2 Ephesians 1:17–2:5   Answer Key

V17 In V16 Paul says that he mentions the Ephesians in what?
   In my prayers.
Paul is going to tell us what he prays for people whom he has heard what two things about? (V15)
   1. *Faith in the Lord Jesus.*
   2. *Love for God's people.*
Paul uses 2 descriptions for God, what are they?
   1. *God of our Lord Jesus Christ.*
   2. *Father of glory.*

Complete this sentence: "may give unto you the __spirit__ of __wisdom__ and __revelation__ in the __knowledge__ of __Him__."

Is the word "spirit" speaking of the Holy Spirit or man's spirit?
   Man's spirit – small "s".
Doesn't **verse 8** say they already had wisdom? <u>Yes</u> or No

Where did the wisdom from **V8** come from? Learning, Mankind, or <u>God</u>.

In **verse 17**, Paul prays for the Ephesians to have wisdom and revelation in what?
   The knowledge of God.   ***See Digging Deeper.
Paul prays for them to have wisdom and knowledge of whom?
   God.

V18 Paul wants the "eyes" of the Ephesians what to be enlightened?
   Understanding.
Paul wants this so that they will know three things, name the first one listed:
   Hope of His calling.
Look up the word "hope" in any source and give its meaning:
   Vine's Expository Dictionary says hope is "favorable and confident expectation."
Whose calling is Paul talking about?
   God's.
What is the second thing Paul wants the Ephesians to know?
   The riches of the glory of His inheritance in the saints.

Look up the word "riches" in any source and give its meaning:
Strong's Exhaustive Concordance Greek meaning – "Wealth, abundance of external possessions, fullness, a good with which one is enriched."

Who is the "his" in this statement?
God.

What is it that is his?
The inheritance.

Where is this inheritance?
In the saints.

Do you have this inheritance? <u>Yes</u> or No   How do you know?
The Bible tells me so.

V19 There is one more thing Paul wants the Ephesians to know, what is that?
The exceeding greatness of his power.

To whom is the "his" in this verse that this power belongs?
God.

To whom is this power going toward?
Us who believe.

Who would <u>not</u> be included in receiving this power?
Unbelievers.

The phrase "according to" in this verse means "in keeping with or in agreement with." This power that believers receive is "in agreement with" what?

KJV *The working of His mighty power.*
AOV

Can you give some examples of what God's power working through believers has already done?   (Try to list at least two)
1. *God's power healed many people. Smith Wigglesworth and Andrew Wommack have raised people from the dead.*
2. *Changes the atmosphere as we bring God's power into the darkness.*
    *** *See Digging Deeper.*

V20 What was it that was "wrought or at work" in Christ?
This same power that is in us.

There are two things listed here that the power of God did in Christ. Name the first one:
Raised Christ from the dead.

Write below how you would explain to someone what it means to "raise someone from the dead." (Make it so simple that a child could understand it)
As we put our complete trust in God and His ability, we can use the power that he has given us and speak to a problem or someone who is dead and tell life to come back into their body.

What is the second thing listed that the power of God did in Christ?
Set him at His own right hand.

Whose power did these things?
God's.

According to verse 19, where is this power at this present time?
In believers.

V21 According to this verse, is this power under, below, level with, above or <u>*far above*</u> all things?

Paul lists a breakdown of the entities that this power is far above. List them below:
1. *Principalities.*
2. *Powers.*
3. *Might.*
4. *Dominion.*
5. *Every name.*

Is the above list of entities for or against God?
Against.

In your opinion, would God use his power to further these or destroy them?
Destroy them because they are against God.

Read Colossians 2:15 What did Christ do to these principalities and powers?
Triumphed over them. ***See Digging Deeper.

Back to Ephesians 1:19 According to this verse, where is this power at this present time?
In believers.

Pick from the following all that apply regarding this power:
- This power could only be used when Christ was on earth.
- This power can be used by everybody, at any time.
- *This power is God's power.*
- *This power is now in believers who have Christ in them.*
- *This power is far above things in this world.*
- This power does not work on situations I encounter in my life.
- *Things of this world are far below this power.*
- *Things in the future are far below this power.*
- *This is the same power Jesus used to defeat the enemy by setting people free when he walked this earth.*
- *This same power is in me. (Say it out Loud!!)*

V22 To whom is the "his" and "him" that this verse is referring? (v20 gives a clue)
Christ.

What two things did God do in Christ?
1. *Put all things under Christ's feet.*
2. *Gave him to be head over all things to the church.*

How many things are under Christ's feet?
All.

God made Christ the head over how many things?
All.

For whose benefit did God do these two things in Christ?
Believers – the church.

In your opinion, who or what is the church?
Those who choose to have Jesus as their Savior and Lord.

V23 Who is the "his" and "him" in this verse?
Christ.

Who is "his" body?
The church.

Paul says the church is what?
The fullness of him.

Look up the word "fullness" and give its meaning:
***See Digging Deeper.**

Read John 1:1 What was in the beginning?
The Word.

This Word was two things at the beginning. What are they?
1. *Was with God.*
2. *Was God.*

Read John 1:14 What happened to the Word?
It became flesh.

Read John 1:16 What is it that we have received?
Of his fullness and grace for grace.

Personally, for you, what does it mean to you to be the fullness of Christ or what does that fullness of Christ look like in your life?
Living like Christ. Fulfilling Mark 16:15-21 Healing the sick, raising the dead, spreading the Good News of the gospel.

Ephesians 2:1 Who is the "you" in this verse?
Believers.

Does this verse indicate something present or *past*?

What were these people?
Dead in their trespasses and sins.

Read Ephesians 1:20 Was Christ dead at one time? *Yes* or No

What happened to Christ?
He was raised from the dead.

Ephesians 2:1 Now what has Christ done for us who were also dead?
Quickened or given us life.

Look up the meaning of the word "quickened" and write it below:
Strong's Exhaustive Concordance Greek meaning - "To exist" (make alive or give life).

V2 What time period is this scripture talking about?
In time past.

Is this scripture for all Christians, only the Ephesians or only those who received the letter in Paul's day?
All Christians.

This verse shows what happened before believers knew Christ. Write below the three things that influenced believers prior to knowing Christ:
1. *Walking according to the course of this world.*
2. *According to the prince of the power of the air.*
3. *According to the spirit that now works in the children of disobedience.*

What did Paul call the being who rules this world?
KJV *Prince of the power of the air*   AOV _____

Where is this power at work now?
    Working in the children of disobedience.
In your opinion, who are the children of disobedience?
    Unbelievers who are under satan's rule.

V3 Who would the "we all" be in this verse?
    All believers.
Is this verse talking about the <u>past</u>, present or future?

How does the KJV list how we lived our lives in the past?
1. *Lusts of the flesh.*
2. *Fulfilling the desires of the flesh and the mind.*

How does AOV list how we lived our lives in the past?
1.
2.

What does each bible version say these children were?
KJV *The children of wrath*   AOV _____

Are you children of wrath or punishment now? Yes or <u>No</u>? Give a reason for your answer?
    Because I accepted what Jesus did for me in taking my punishment and satisfying God's wrath.

V4 God was rich in what, according to this verse?
    Mercy.
God loved us with what, according to this verse?
    His Great Love.

V5 When was it that God loved us?
>   When we were perfect.
>   When we were forgiven from all our sins.
>   When we were going to church.
>   <u>When we were dead in sin or in the middle of doing wrong.</u>

What did God do when we were dead in sin?
KJV *Quickened us together with Him.*
AOV

Did God do this because we earned it by our actions or anything that we had done? Yes or <u>No</u>

How could this have happened, that when we were children of punishment, deserving of God's wrath and committing sins, that we were made alive with Christ? Write out below the words in parentheses from the KJV of **verse 5**:
>   *By grace ye are saved.*

Explain as best you can what that phrase "by grace ye are saved" means:
>   *Nothing I can do or did or ever will do, will save me from destruction*
>   *or God's wrath. Only by God's abundant grace through what Jesus Christ*
>   *has done for me in his death, burial and resurrection can I ever be saved*
>   *or set free from the blinding power of the enemy.*

NOTES

Worksheet 3 - Ephesians 2:6 – 22   Answer Key

V6 From **verse 4**, who is the being that has performed what this verse says?
   God

From **verses 5 and 6** there are three things that God did for us <u>together</u> in Christ. Name them:
1. *Quickened us or gave us life.*
2. *Raised us up.*
3. *Made us sit in heavenly places.*

Where is Christ raised up to?
   Heavenly places.
Where is Christ seated?
   In heavenly places.

Read Ephesians 1:20 More specifically, where is Christ seated?
   At God's right hand in heavenly places.

Ephesians 2:6 Is this verse telling us that at this very moment, we are also made alive, raised up and seated where Christ is? <u>Yes</u> or No
   This is the supreme position of authority. Having all things under our feet is because of our position in Christ.

Read Colossians 3:1 What are we suppose to do because of our position in Christ or because of who Christ has made us?
   Set our hearts on things above.

Try to name three things that are above that we should be seeking?
1. *The fullness of the operation of the Kingdom of God.*
2. *No sickness, disease, hurt, pain, negative thoughts or actions.*
3. *Experience relationship with the Father and Jesus.*

   ****See Digging Deeper.*

Ephesians 2:7 This verse is God's purpose in doing those three things. Write out this verse below from the KJV:
   That in the ages to come, he (God) might shew the exceeding riches of his grace in his kindness toward us through Christ Jesus.

What words does AOV use for "the ages to come"?
Future generations.
What words does the KJV use to describe the intensity of God's grace?
Exceeding Riches.
God showed this grace by what?
His Kindness.
Through whom?
Jesus Christ.

V8 Look up the meanings of the following: Merriam Webster's online Dictionary
By   *"Through or through the means of, via."*
Through   *"In one side and out the other, movement within a place or area."*

There are two things in this verse that are necessary to become saved, fill in the blanks with those things:
By _____*Grace*_____   Through _____*Faith*_____

Read Ephesians 3:7 Tells us about grace. <u>Is it a gift</u> or is it earned?
<u>Is it of God</u> or of man?

Read Titus 2:11 What is it that the grace of God does?
Brings salvation.
Read Romans 10:17 How does faith come?
By hearing.

Ephesians 2:9 What does the phrase "not of works" mean to you?
I cannot perform any works or obedience to the law to earn the gift of grace or salvation.
Why is it important to know that nothing man did caused him to be saved?
So that man wouldn't boast about his greatness.

V10 There are two things listed here that we are because we are saved. What are they?
1. *We are his workmanship.*
2. *Created in Christ Jesus.*

What does it mean to be someone's workmanship?
Mankind was made or formed by God through Jesus.
For what were we created?
Good works.

Are these good works that we have decided to do or _God has prepared for us to do_?

Are these good works done once in a while, once a week, when we feel like it or _is it how we live our daily lives_?

These good works are a result of God's workmanship that is where?
In Christ Jesus. Jesus' life is our earthly example of good works.
When did God decide to make us his workmanship in order to house Christ Jesus?
Before ordained.
Read Romans 9:23 What is God making known?
The riches of his glory.
Who is God's glory being make known toward?
The vessels of mercy.
When did God decide to do this?
Before ordained.
In your opinion, what do you think the "riches of his glory" would be?
The extreme goodness of His personality and presence.

Ephesians 2:11 Fill in the blanks: "Wherefore __remember__, that ye being _in_ _time_ _past_ _Gentiles_ in _the_ _flesh_, who are called __uncircumcision__ by that which is _called_ the __circumcision__ in the _flesh_ _made_ _by_ _hands_;"

Who are the circumcised? ____Jews____
Who are the uncircumcised? ____Gentiles____

What is it that Paul wants them to remember?
That they were once Gentiles in the flesh.

V12 What time is Paul talking about at the beginning of this verse? (V11 will give you the answer)
When they were Gentiles and didn't serve God.

At that time, what were they without?
Christ.

There are four things listed here that are the consequences of not having Christ in their lives, list them:
1. *Alien's from the commonwealth or being citizens of Israel.*
2. *Strangers from the covenant of promise.*
3. *With no hope.*
4. *Without God in the world.*

V13 What changed to make them not those four things from the last verse?
Now they have received what God had done for them through Christ.
What were they before?
Far off or far away from God.
What has happen now because of Christ?
They have become near.
How did that happen?
By the blood of Christ.

V14 What is Jesus Christ?
Our peace.
There are two things that Jesus Christ our peace did, list them:
1. *He made both one.*
2. *Broke the wall between them.*
What two groups is this verse talking about?
Children & Adults, You & your neighbors, <u>Jew & Gentile.</u>

V15 What did Christ destroy in his flesh?
The enmity.
Look up the word "enmity" in any source and give its meaning:
Vine's says enmity is "hatred, it is the opposite of agape." Agape is God's love.
In destroying the enmity something else was also destroyed, what was that?
The law of commandments contained in ordinances.
What was God creating in Christ by destroying the enmity and laws?
Making one new man out of two groups.
What was the ultimate result?
Peace.

V16 What was Jesus' purpose for making these two people groups one?
To reconcile both groups into one.

How was this accomplished?
> *By the cross.*

What was slain or killed or ended because of what was done at the cross?
> *The enmity.*

V17 Is this verse still talking about what Jesus has accomplished? <u>Yes</u> or No

What does this verse say that Jesus did to them?
> *Preached peace.*

To what two groups did he preach peace?
1. *Those who were far off.*
2. *Those who were near.*

What does AOV call "the enmity"?
> *Detailed rules of the law. (V15)*

V18 Through Jesus, what was accomplished?
1. They could all get together and build a church building.
2. They could all sacrifice animals and obey laws together.
3. <u>*They could all have access to the Father by one and the same Spirit.*</u>

Whose spirit gives Jew and Gentile access to the Father?
> *Holy Spirit.*

V19 The results of what the Father did through Jesus for the Jews and Gentiles are that they are no longer what?

1. *Strangers*   2. *Foreigners*

But they are these two things:

1. *Fellow citizens.*   2. *Saints.*

V20 Look up the word "foundation" in any source and give its meaning:
> *Greek meaning is "beginnings or first principles."*

What was the foundation of the Ephesians built upon?
> *(Teachings of) apostles and prophets.*

Who was the chief cornerstone of that foundation?
> *Jesus Christ.*

V21 Who is the "whom" in this verse?
> *Jesus Christ.*

What is fitly framed or joined together in Christ?
> *All the building.*

Who does the phrase "all the building" represent?
Jew and Gentile, followers of Christ.
What does the building grow into?
A holy temple.
What was the purpose of the building called the temple in the Old Testament?
It was a place to meet God.
Read 1 Corinthians 3:16 Paul is talking to believers. Who is he telling them they are?
The temple.
What dwells in them?
The Spirit of God.

V22 Who is the "whom" in this verse?
Jesus Christ.
They are what?
Built together.
For what purpose?
A habitation of God.
Look up the word "habitation" and give its meaning: Merriam Webster's
online dictionary says habitation is "a place where someone lives."
How does this habitation of God happen?
Through the Spirit.
What spirit is this verse talking about, man's spirit or <u>God's Spirit</u>?

***See Digging Deeper: Salvation and Faith.*

Worksheet 4 Ephesians 3:1–3:15 Answer Key

V1 What is the first statement Paul makes in this verse, prior to stating his name?
  For this cause.

Read Ephesians 2:19-22 (you can go back further if you want) and write below how you would describe what Paul means by the statement "for this cause"?
1. *No more strangers but citizens of God's household.*
2. *Built upon the apostles and prophets teachings.*
3. *We all are built together as God's Holy temple.*
4. *The Gentiles are now accepted into God's family and treated the same as everyone else.*

What does Paul call himself in this verse?
  The prisoner.
For whom is Paul a prisoner?
  The Gentiles.
In what city was Paul a prisoner? (Acts 28:16)
  Rome.

V2 What was it that the Ephesians had heard?
  The dispensation of the grace of God.
Look up the word "dispensation" from any source and give its meaning:
  Greek meaning: "management of household affairs."
Who was given this message?
  Paul.
For whom was Paul given the message?
  The Gentiles.

V3 How did Paul receive this message?
  By revelation.
Who made known this revelation message to Paul?
  God.
What does Paul call this message in each version?
KJV ____*The mystery*____ AOV _____

Had Paul told them about this mystery *before*, or was this the only time?

V4 What were the Ephesians going to understand when they read what Paul had written before?

His knowledge of the mystery of Christ.

V5 Was there ever a time when this mystery was not known by the sons of men?   Yes.

 When was that?

KJV ___*Other ages*_____   AOV _____

Who are the "sons of men"?

Humans.

Is this being revealed now as it was in Paul's day?

Yes.

Who is the mystery being revealed to in this verse?

Holy apostles and prophets.

How is this mystery being revealed to them?

By the Spirit.

Read Galatians 1:12 How was this mystery made known unto Paul?

By a revelation of Jesus Christ.

Look up the word "revelation" and give its meaning:

Greek meaning: "take the cover off." That means that it was always there and is getting revealed by Jesus. (The Old Testament attests to that.)

Ephesians 3:6 This describes the mystery that Paul is talking about. There are three main points to this mystery, write them below:

1. *Gentiles be fellow heirs.*
2. *Gentiles are of the same body.*
3. *Gentiles partake of His promise in Christ.*

Who is the "his" in this verse?

God.

Where is this promise?

In Christ.

In your opinion, describe what you think the gospel is?

The good news that Jesus Christ became man to suffer my punishment and take God's wrath so that I could have a loving relationship with my loving heavenly Father.

V7 Who is the "I" in this verse?

Paul.

What was Paul made?
   A minister.
Look up the word "minister" in any source and give its meaning?
   Greek meaning: "to carry out the commands of another."
By what was Paul made a minister?
   The gift of grace.
How was this gift given unto Paul?
   By the effectual working of God's power.
Look up the word "effectual" in any source and give its meaning:
   Greek meaning: energeia – *"superhuman power."*
   Merriam Webster's online dictionary: *"accomplishment of a desired result."*
Is this verse saying that the gift of grace Paul received from God was given because of God's power that accomplishes what it is sent to accomplish, which in this verse, is to make Paul a minister of the gospel? <u>Yes</u> or No

V8 How does Paul explain himself in this verse?
   Less than the least of all the saints.
What was given to him?
   Grace.
Paul a minster or called to preach to whom?
   Gentiles.
Is Paul a Gentile? Yes or <u>No</u>. If No, then what is he? *Jew.*

What is the message that Paul is given the grace to preach?
KJV <u>*Unsearchable riches of Christ*</u>   AOV _____

V9 There is more to what Paul has been called by God to do. What must he make all men see?
   The fellowship of the mystery.
How long has this mystery been hidden?
   From the beginning of the world.
Where has this mystery been hidden?
   In God.
Write out the next statement about God that starts with "who
_____<u>*Created all things by Jesus Christ.*</u>_____

Read Isaiah 44:24 Who does Isaiah say is speaking in this verse?
   The Lord, thy redeemer.

Who does God say created all things?
> *He did.*

When you compare Isaiah 44:24 to Ephesians 3:9 is Jesus Christ deity or God?
> *Yes* or No

John 1:1-3 V2 Where was the Word in the beginning?
> *With God.*

V3 Was anything made without the Word or without Jesus? Yes or *No*

Ephesians 3:10 What time frame is this verse addressing? (pick all that apply)
> Prior to Jesus, *In Paul's day*, *After Jesus' death*, In Old Testament times, *Currently in our time*.

What is it that is being made known?
KJV *The manifold wisdom of God* AOV _____

Who is making this known?
> *The church.*

The church is making this known to whom?
> *The principalities and powers.*

Who would you say are the "principalities and powers in heavenly places"?
> *Demons*   ***See Digging Deeper.

V11 God's plan to make his wisdom known to principalities and powers through the church was according to:
1. A momentary thought.
2. An idea by the angels.
3. *A plan from the beginning of time.*

This plan was accomplished through whom?
> *Christ Jesus our Lord.*

V12 Who is the "whom" this verse is talking about?
> *Christ Jesus.*

Who is the "we" this verse is talking about?
> *The church or believers.*

What 2 things does this verse say the "we" have?
1. *Boldness.*
    ***See Digging Deeper.
2. *Access.*

How is the "we" able to possess those two things?
   With boldness.
Who is the "him" in this verse?
   Christ Jesus.

V13 Because the "we" have boldness and confident access to God, what is it that Paul desires for them <u>NOT</u> to do? (Pick one)
   Run, jump, have courage, <u>faint</u>, have boldness.
What phrase is used in AOV for "faint not"?
   Become discouraged.
At what are "we" not to faint?
   Paul's tribulations.
On behalf of whom does Paul say he goes through these things?
   The church or believers.
On behalf of what does Paul say it benefits those for whom he goes through this?
   For their glory.
   *** *See Digging Deeper.*

2 Corinthians 11:23-28 Name six of the things that Paul went through to bring the gospel to believers:
1. *Fastings.*
2. *Watching.*
3. *Nakedness.*
4. *Three times ship-wrecked.*
5. *Perils.*
6. *Care of the churches.*

Ephesians 3:14 Paul says "For this cause" to begin this verse. To what cause is he referring? (v13)
   Tribulations.
What do we call what Paul is doing?
   Prayer.
To whom is Paul bowing his knee?
   The Father of our Lord Jesus.

V15 Paul uses the words "the whole family" in this verse. Who do you think "the whole family" represents?
   Believers.
From where is the whole family represented?
   Heaven and earth.

What is it that the whole family has received?
　　A name.
Are you named with the same name that they have received? <u>Yes</u> or No

Read Philippians 2:9-11 What is the name that is higher than any other name?
　　The name of Jesus.
What must bow to that name?
1. *Every knee of things in heaven.*
2. *Every knee of things in earth.*
3. *Every knee of things under the earth.*

Would what Paul is about to pray apply to you? <u>Yes</u> or No

　　Be sure to read and meditate on what Paul is praying from the next
　　　　　　Worksheet. Ephesians 3:16-21

Worksheet 5 Ephesians 3:16 – 4:10 Answer Key

V16 Who is the "he" in this verse?   *The Father.*

Who is the "you" in this verse?   *Believers/Ephesians.*

  Paul is praying "according to" or based on what?
    The riches of His glory.

What would you think the statement "according to the riches of his glory" means?
    The fullness of his presence felt in the believers heart as he experiences the love of God. Seeing God's love displayed as someone receives healing, miracles or a touch on someone's life.

What does Paul desire for them to be?
    Strengthened with might.

What is the source of this might or power?
    The Holy Spirit.

Where does Paul desire this to happen?
    In the inner man.

Read 2 Corinthians 4:16 This verse is speaking about two parts of a man. List them below:
1. *Outward man – perishing.*
2. *Inward man – being renewed day by day.*

Next to each part of man above write what is happening to each according to this verse.

What man is Paul talking about in **Ephesians 3:16**?
    Inner man   *** See Digging Deeper.

Ephesians 3:17 Where does Paul pray that Christ would dwell?
    In our/their hearts.

How does Paul pray that Christ would dwell in their hearts?
    By faith opposed to feeling.

How would you describe to someone what "faith" is?
    Unwavering trust in God. Believing He is who He says He is, I am who He says I am and He has done what He said He would do and I can have everything that He said I can have.

Does Christ already dwell in the believer? <u>Yes</u> or No

If yes, then in what part of the believer does Christ dwell?
    Spirit.

Give a reason why Paul would pray that Christ would dwell in them if Christ already dwells in the believer?
Though our spirit already houses Christ, our inner man (soul) does not and needs to be renewed to the things of Christ. Life is not about us living for Christ but about us yielding to the Spirit in us and allowing Christ's life to live through us.

Complete this statement "that __ye__, being __rooted__ and __grounded__ in __love__."

In your opinion, what do each of the words below mean:
Rooted __*Greek meaning: "to cause to strike out or establish"*__
Grounded __*Greek meaning: "to lay the foundation"*__

V18 What does Paul pray for them to be able to do?
Comprehend.
Look up the word "comprehend" in any source and give its meaning:
Greek meaning: "to lay hold as if to make it your own. Take possession."

Who else does Paul include that are able to comprehend?
All the saints.

Paul lists four areas of what he desires them to comprehend. List them below:
1. *Breadth – width* 2. *Length – long*
3. *Depth – deep* 4. *Height – high*

V19 Pick which best describes what Paul is praying in verses 18 & 19 that he desires for these people:
- To be able to live and do.
- To be able to acknowledge and say.
- *To be able to comprehend and know.*

What does he want them to comprehend and know?
Christ's love.

What is the description Paul uses in regard to this love?
- It is never ending.
- It is placed in man by cupid.
- It is a warm and cozy feeling.
- *It passes knowledge.*

Paul says that by comprehending and knowing the love of Christ the result would be what?
Being filled with all the fullness of God.

So, if we Christians want to be filled with God's fullness, then these verses tell us that we must have an understanding and knowledge of Christ's love?
    Yes or No

V20 Who do you think the "him" is in this verse? (v14 is a hint)
    The Father.
Paul uses two verbs to describe what the Father can do. Give their meanings below:
Exceeding: *Greek meaning: "over, beyond, more than."*
Abundantly: *Greek meaning: "more than is necessary, superior, uncommon."*
               Merriam Websters online dictionary: "over sufficient."

Is what "he" can do between, below or above according to this verse?
    Above.
What can "he" do exceeding and abundantly above?
    All that we ask or think.
He does this according to what?
      According to how the world's economy is going at the time.
      According to what the government says.
      According to the power that works in us.

Where is this power?
    Working in us.
As best you can, explain where we got this power?
    Acts 1:8 From the Holy Spirit.

V21 Fill in the blanks: "Unto __Him__ be __glory__ in the __church__ by __Christ__ __Jesus__ throughout all __ages__, __world__ without __end__. __Amen__."
Where is this glory?
    In the church.
How does the church make known this glory?
    By spreading the good news through healing, setting people free from worldly bondage.
How long will the church be making this glory known?
KJV __World without end__   AOV _____
    *** *See Digging Deeper.*

V4:1 What does Paul call himself in this verse?
    A prisoner for the Lord.

What does Paul encourage the readers of this letter to do?
KJV *Walk worthy of the vocation.* AOV *Live as people worthy of the call.*

Which statement would best describe how believers are to live?
1. The same way they did before Christ came to live in them.
2. *As people who honor what God has done for them by their actions.*

V2 Paul lists four ways that will enable the church to live worthy of the call of God. List them below:

KJV	AOV
1. *Lowliness.*	1. *Humility.*
2. *Meekness.*	2. *Gentleness.*
3. *Long-suffering.*	3. *Patience.*
4. *Forbearing one another.*	4. *Accepting each other with love.*

V3 What is it that Paul asks the readers to make every effort to keep?
The unity of the Spirit.
What Spirit is Paul talking about? Our spirit or <u>the Holy Spirit</u>.

How is this unity kept or continued in believers lives?
KJV <u>*In the bond of peace*</u>   AOV <u>*Peace that ties you together*</u>

Who do you think this peace is between?
Believers

V4 & 5 Paul is making statements of truths or absolutes that are essential to the unity of the church, Christ's body. List them below:
1. *One body – In Jesus Christ.*
2. *One Spirit – the Holy Spirit giving us life.*
3. *One hope of calling – Receiving Christ, becoming like him, and spreading the gospel.*
4. *One Lord – Who is our master into whose image we are transformed.*
5. *One faith – In Jesus Christ and his atonement.*
6. *One baptism – Into Jesus Christ.*

V6 What is the last statement of truth or absolute that Paul mentions?
One God and Father of all.
Where does this verse state that this absolute truth resides?
1. *Over all – believers.*
2. *Through all – believers. Paul is talking to believers not the world.*
3. *In all - believers.*

V7 What is given unto us?
Grace.
How would you explain to someone what "grace is" ?
Favor and the power of God for living in righteousness.

This grace that we have been given is in regards to what?
- How many commandments we obey.
- How often we forgive others.
- *The measure of the gift of Christ.*

How much did you receive of Christ? (Pick one.)
A little, just enough to get by, *everything we need for every situation we will every encounter.*

V8 Read Psalm 68:18. What are the three things listed here that Christ did?
1. *Ascended on high.*
2. *Led captivity captive.*
3. *Received gifts for men.*

The last portion of this verse tells why these three things were done. What does it say?
So that the Lord would dwell among them.

Ephesians 4:9 & 10 This phrase gives more description regarding the quote from Psalm 68:18.
Who is the "he" in these verses?
Christ.
What happen first before he ascended?
He descended.
To where did he descend?
The lower parts of the earth.

Read 1 Peter 3:19 & 4:6
V19 What does Peter call the place that Paul called the "lower parts of the earth?" (pick one)
A palace, a home, *a prison*, a resting place?

1 Peter 4:6 What did Jesus do while he was in that prison, to those who were there?
Preached the gospel.
Peter gives two reasons why the gospel needed to be preached to those in that prison or the lower part of the earth. List them below:

1. *So they would be judged as men of the earth.*
2. *Live according to God in the spirit.*
   Every person ever born before Jesus' life on earth, was presented with the truth of the gospel and made a choice which to accept. All spirits live on in whatever place they have chosen.   Luke 16:23-30

Read John 5:24-29

V28 Where does this verse say that Jesus will preach or where will they hear his voice? (pick one)

> On earth, in the synagogue, in churches, *in the graves*.

V29 There are two types of resurrection listed that the hearers will be a part of. List them below:
1. *Resurrection of life.*
2. *Resurrection of damnation.*

Go back to Ephesians 4:10 How far did Jesus ascend?
> *Far above all.*

What reason did Paul give for Jesus descending and ascending?
> *That he might fill all in all.*

Look up the word "fill" in any source and give its meanings:
> *Greek Lexicon: pleroo Christ fills by being "exalted to share in the divine administration, He is said to fill (pervade) the universe with his presence, power and activity." Christians fill by "being those who are pervaded (richly furnished) with the power and gifts of the Holy Spirit, rooted, in Christ by virtue of the intimate relationship entered into with Him."*

During this week: Pray the prayer that Paul prayed for the Ephesians (3:16-21) with thankfulness, for someone in your life. Pray for a different person or more than one, every day. Be sure to journal who you prayed for this week so you can have a praise report to share with other believers.

Worksheet 6 Ephesians 4:11-27 Answer Key

V11 From the last worksheet, we know that God has given the church gifts. There are five listed here:
1. *Apostles – someone sent forth with orders.*
2. *Prophets – a spokesman for God by inspiration.*
3. *Evangelists – bringers of good news that are not apostles.*
4. *Pastors – a shepherd. A New Testament shepherd was responsible for watching over, defending from attack, healing, loving and gaining the trust of the sheep.*
5. *Teachers – helping others to learn with the help of the Holy Spirit.*

V12 There are three benefits for these gifts. List them below:
1. *Perfecting the saints – Giving them equipment to minister.*

2. *For the work of the ministry – The Great Commission from Mark 16:14-20.*

3. *For the edifying of the body of Christ. - Promoting the growth of believers.*

Next to each benefit above, explain in your own words what you think each means.

Who is being equipped or perfected to minister and edify the body of Christ? Mankind, Angels, *Believers*, Unbelievers, *Saints*.   (Pick all that apply)

V13 There are two results that this perfecting is to accomplish. List them below:
1. *Unity of the faith.*
2. *Knowledge of the Son of God.*

These two results will create what type of man?
   Perfect man.
The remainder of this verse describes what that type of man is.
Is he:
   1. Just starting to grow   2. Partially grown but have a long way to go
   3. *Fully grown.*
What measure does AOV say is used to show this full growth?
   By the fullness of Christ.

Look at Ephesians 3:16-19

In Paul's prayer for the Ephesians, he wants them to be strengthened by the Spirit, to know that Christ dwells in them, to be rooted and grounded in love, and to be able to comprehend and know the love of Christ so that what can happen in them?   *To be filled with the fullness of God.*

When that prayer is compared with **Ephesians 4:13** what is the end result that Paul wants the Ephesians and the saints to know?
We should house the fullness of God and all he is, as mature followers so that whatever we do for the kingdom will be effective, producing results for God's glory or to honor him.

V14 This verse explains what happens to believers who do <u>not</u> know for themselves that end result. What does it say they are:

      Beggars, sinners, <u>children</u>, saints.

What word does AOV use for the previous answer?
  Infants.
The KJV lists four traits of this type of person. List them below:
1. *Tossed to and fro.*
2. *Carried away with every wind of doctrine.*
3. *By the slight of men.*
4. *And with cunning craftiness.*

What does the KJV say that people are trying to do, by these traits, to others?
1. Have faith in God.
2. Grow in the knowledge of what Christ has done for us.
3. <u>*Lie in wait to deceive.*</u>

V15 What are the saints or believers suppose to speak?
   The truth in or with love.
What does it cause believers to do when they speak the truth in love?
   They grow up into him in all things.
This verse says we are to grow into what?
   Into Christ.
This verse says that Christ is what?
   The head.

Read Colossians 2:19. Who would Christ be in this verse?
The head.

There are three things listed here that the Head does for the body, what are they?
1. *Gets nourishment.*
2. *Knits together.*
3. *Increases with the increase of God.*

Because of what this verse says, can we conclude that everything that a believer needs to live life, have unity with other saints and be filled with God's fullness, comes from the head? *Yes* or No

V16 This verse is describing who as the head?
Christ.

What grows from the head?
The whole body.

Write Verse 16 from AOV: _____
_____
_____
_____
_____
_____

This verse is talking about the body of Christ growing. *True* or False

Does each part of the body need to work in order for the body to grow?
Yes.

When every part of the body is effectually working what is edified or built up?
Others that meet the body or *the body itself.*

What does the body of Christ have to do to grow?
Edify itself in love.

V17 Paul is telling believers not to live life as whom?
The Gentiles.

V17, 18, 19 Next to each breakdown of the traits of others Gentiles below, write the equivalent from AOV.
1. "the vanity of their mind" _Pointless thinking._
2. "having the understanding darkened" _Dark in their reasoning._
3. "alienated from the life of God through ignorance" _Disconnected from God's life because of their ignorance._
4. "the blindness of their heart" _Having a closed or hardened heart._
5. "being past feeling" _Lost all sense of right and wrong._
6. "given over to lasciviousness" _Given themselves over to whatever feels good._
7. "work all uncleaness with greediness" _Practicing every sort of corruption along with greed._

V20 Who is the "ye" or "you" in this verse?
   Believers.
Who does this verse say that they did not learn the things in verse 17, 18, 19 from?
   Christ.

V21 This verse lists two ways in which they have learned from Christ. List them below:
1. *Listened to him.*
2. *Have been taught by him.*

What is in Christ?
   The truth.
If you need to know what things are truth, where would you look to find it?
   Look at Jesus' life.
Look up the word "truth" or "true" in any source and give its meaning.
   Merriam Webster's online dictionary: "Real facts about something."

John 8:31-32 "Then said Jesus to those Jews which believed on him, If ye continue in my word, *then* are ye my disciples indeed; And ye shall know the truth, and the truth shall make you free."

From the verses above, what did Jesus say that disciples do to show they are disciples?
   Continue in His word.
What is gained by continuing in or abiding in the word?
   You will know the truth.

What does knowledge of the truth do?
  Makes you free.
If we know people who are not free, what are they lacking?
  Knowledge of the truth.

V22 From the following portions of this verse write the same from AOV:
1. "put off" ___*Change.*___
2. "former coversation" ___*The former way of life.*___
3. "the old man" ___*The part of the person you once were.*___
4. "corrupt" ___*Corrupted.*___
5. "deceitful lusts" ___*Deceitful desires.*___

When were you that old man?
  Before I asked Jesus into my life.
V23 What needs to happen to put off the former way of life?
  Be reborn, be redeemed, be received, be renewed, be righteous.

Where does this renewal take place?
  In the spirit of your mind. We must have a renewed mental disposition.
V24 From the following portions of this verse write the same from AOV:
1. "put on" ___*Clothe yourself.*___
2. "new man" ___*New person.*___
3. "which after God is created" ___*According to God's image.*___
4. "righteousness" ___*Justice.*___
5. "true holiness" ___*True holiness.*___

Who was your new person created to be like?
  God. To think like, act like and respond like God.
How did **verse 23** say we are to put on this new person?
1. By praying morning, noon and night.   2. By showing love to others.
3. *By renewing our minds.*   4. Being involved in the church.

In your opinion, to what do believers renew their minds?
  Who we are in Christ after the death, burial and resurrection of Jesus.
Write below ways in which you renew your mind?
  Meditating scripture – rolling it over in our minds, matching it with
  other scripture until we clearly understand what is being said.

V25 This scripture begins Paul's examples of practical applications of the new man. Who would these apply to?
    Believers.

What is the first thing Paul says to "put away"?
    Lying, anything opposing God.

What is the opposite or right way to handle the first thing Paul mentions?
    Speak the truth with your neighbor.

Where does truth come from? (**V21**)
    Jesus.

What reason does Paul give for this practical application?
    We are members of one body.

Who would be the neighbor that Paul is talking about?
    Other believers.

V26 What is the next practical application?
    Be angry.

Is this commanding us to <u>be angry</u> or not be angry?
    Past teaching has told us this means that we can be angry as long as we aren't angry in the morning, but it clearly says be angry. Let's look at other scripture to see what we are to be angry with.

Read Psalm 97:10. What are we to hate or have intense dislike for?
    Evil.

In your opinion, At whom should our anger be directed?
    Satan, devil, demons, injustice, wickedness.

At whom should our anger <u>not</u> be directed?
    Human beings.

If we are ever angry, we should only be angry at the following?
(Pick all that apply)
    <u>Demons</u>, your neighbor, the sales clerk, your spouse, <u>evil</u>, <u>injustice</u>, <u>satan</u>.

Ephesians 4:26 Are we ever to sin?   Yes or <u>No</u>

What happens when the sun goes down?
1. <u>Our human bodies want to relax.</u>
2. <u>It is time for human bodies to rest.</u>
3. <u>Human bodies sleep.</u>

The KJV says "let not" at the beginning of this phrase, what does AOV say?
Don't let.
Who is responsible to let or not let something to happen in your life?
We are.
If a Christian were to relax or allow his anger against the enemy, the devil, to sleep, would it be possible for the devil to get an open door or influence into a Christian's life and that influence might cause them to forget who they are or sin in some area?
<u>Yes</u> or No

Ephesians 4:27 What does AOV say for the words "neither give place" from the KJV?
Don't provide an opportunity.
To whom are we <u>not</u> to give place?
The devil.
In your opinion, which of the following would give place to the devil?
1. <u>Holding on to an offense</u>.
2. <u>Being angry with a neighbor or family member.</u>
3. <u>Degrading or speaking bad about yourself or someone else</u>.
4. <u>Being fearful, anxious or worried about things</u>.
5. <u>Allowing strife or conflict with others in our lives</u>.

Give at least two ways in which you can guard yourself from giving place to the devil:
1. Keep God's Word as first place above all feelings or attitudes.

2. Determine to change, Repent.

   ***See Digging Deeper.*

NOTES

Worksheet 7 Ephesians 4:28 – 5:14 Answer Key

V28 To whom is this verse addressed?
   A thief.
Does a thief *take* or give?

Whose influence is a thief under when he takes?
   Satans.
What type of work does Paul tell them to do?
   Bad, mediocre, just getting by, *good*?

For what purpose does Paul tell them this work is to be done?
   That he may have to give to him that needs.

V29 Write this verse out below from AOV of the Bible. (The Amplified is very descriptive.)

_____
_____
_____
_____
_____
_____
_____

According to this verse, what type of words should we be speaking?
   Good words that edify and minister grace.

Beside each word below write an E for edifying or a C for corrupt next to each that they apply to:

_C_ gossip	_C_ sharing faults of others	_E_ forgiving words
_E_ kind words	_C_ gripping about work	_E_ encouraging words
_C_ mockery	_E_ notice and speak good	_C_ complaining
_C_ criticism	_C_ negative words	_E_ words giving hope

V30 Who is this verse talking about?
   The Holy Spirit of God.
What are we *not* to do to the Holy Spirit?
   Grieve.

Would the things listed in verses 25, 28, 29 and 31 grieve the Holy Spirit?
Yes.
Look up the word "grieve" and give its meaning below:
Greek meaning: "to make sorrowful, affect with sadness."
In regards to the believer, where is the Holy Spirit?
In our spirit.
Until what time is the believer sealed?
The day of redemption.
Have believers spirits already been redeemed? <u>Yes</u> or No

Romans 8:23 What redemption is being spoken of here?
The redemption of our body.
So, what part of us has been redeemed? Body, Soul, <u>*Spirit.*</u>

Ephesians 4:31 List below what is to be put away or stopped in the believers life.
1. *Bitterness.*
2. *Losing your temper.*
3. *Anger.*
4. *Shouting (in anger).*
5. *Slander.*

Paul is saying in this verse, <u>not</u> to be angry and in verse 26 he says to be angry. Are there different types of anger? <u>Yes</u> or No

Explain your answer: *There is a righteous anger at evil and injustice and there is an unrighteous anger at people.*
By the statement "along with every other evil" what is Paul saying that these things are?
Evil.
Who is the author of evil?
Satan.

V32 What three things does Paul tell us to "be"?
1. *Kind.*
2. *Compassionate.*
3. *Forgiving.*

To whom are we to be these things?
Each other - everyone.
In what way are we supposed to do this?
The same way God forgave us.
How much did God forgive us in Christ?
Completely, He forgave all.   ****See Digging Deeper.*

V5:1 Paul's previous instructions can be concluded by telling us to be what of God?
KJV __*Followers*__   AOV __*Imitate*__

Look up the word "imitate" and give its meaning:
Merriam Webster's online dictionary: "To do something the same as something else, to copy someone's behavior"

When we imitate God we do it in what way?
As dearly loved children.

V2 How are we to live our life?
Walk in love.
Who is our example of love?
Christ.
What did he do because of his great love for mankind?
Gave himself.
For whom did he give himself?
Mankind.
Finish this verse: "Hath given himself (who? __*Christ Jesus*__) for us an __*offering*__ and a __*sacrifice*__ to God for a __*sweet*__ __*smelling savour.*__"

What Old Testament procedure would be like this description of what Christ has done for us?
1. Lighting of candles.
2. Placing blood on the altar.
3. Washing in a bowl.
4. *Burnt offering covenant.*

****See Digging Deeper.*

V3 There are three things listed here from the KJV write the equivalent from AOV.
1. Fornication _____*Sexual immorality.*_____
2. All uncleanness ___*Any kind of impurity.*___
3. Covetousness ___*Greed.*_____

Should this be talked about among believers?   Yes or *No*

V4 There are three things listed here from the KJV write the equivalent from AOV.
1. Filthiness _____*Obscene language.*_____
2. Foolish talking ___*Silly talk.*_____
3. Jesting _____*Vulgar jokes.*_____

These types of language are not acceptable or convenient for whom?
   Holy people.

What types of words are believers supposed to say instead?
   Giving of thanks.

V5 There are four things here that Paul assumes that these believers already know. Write the equivalent from AOV.
1. Whoremonger ___*Sexual immorality.*_____
2. Unclean person ___*Impure.*_____
3. Covetous man ___*Greedy.*_____
4. Idolater _____*When things become gods.*_

All these things happen to people when they allow what to happen? (pick one)
1. When they let others lead them astray.
2. When they get too busy and don't read the Word.
3. *When they allow things to become gods in their lives.*

What is it that these people will <u>not</u> receive?
   The kingdom of God.

Let's look at some scriptures where Jesus talks about the Kingdom of God.

Matthew 6:33 What is the first thing Jesus tells his disciples to seek?
The Kingdom of God – not money, clothes or worry about food.

Matthew 12:28 What is one aspect that shows everyone that the Kingdom has come?
Casting out devils by the Kingdom of God.

Mark 4:11 Does this verse imply that the parables of Jesus reveal the Kingdom of God?
Yes.

Mark 10:15 How do believers receive the Kingdom of God?
As little children.

In your opinion, what are some traits of little children?
Children are very trusting, have no fears, quick to believe, total dependence on adults.

Luke 7:28 Who is the greatest prophet ever born?
John the Baptist.

Who is greater than John the Baptist in the Kingdom of God?
The very least saint.

Luke 9:2 Jesus sent the disciples to do what?
Preach the Kingdom of God.

What goes along with preaching the Kingdom?
Healing the sick.

Luke 10:9 Jesus is sending out 70 disciples. What is the first thing he tells them to do?
Heal the sick.

After the sick are healed, what does Jesus tell the 70 disciples to say?
The Kingdom of God has come to you.

Luke 17:20-21 Jesus said the Kingdom of God is where?
Within us.   ***See Digging Deeper.*

Back to Ephesians 5:6 What does Paul warn about in this verse?
To be deceived with vain words.

What does AOV use for *vain words*?
Stupid ideas.

What comes on people who deceive in this way?
Wrath of God.

What are people called who also receive God's wrath?
Children of disobedience.

In your opinion, who are these children of disobedience?
Non-believers because of verse 7.

V7 What does Paul warn believers against in this verse?
Don't be partakers with the children of disobedience.
Look up the word "partake" and pick the answer that best describes the meaning for this verse:
    Don't be like them.
    <u>Don't share in what they are doing.</u>
    Have nothing to do with them.

V8 What were the Ephesians before?
Sometimes darkness.
What are they now?
Light in the Lord.
How are they to live or walk?
As children of light.

John 8:12 Who is the light?
Jesus.

Matthew 5:14 Who else called believers "light"?
Jesus.

John 9:5 What did Jesus say about who he was while on this earth?
The light of the world.
Is that light still visible now on this earth? <u>Yes</u> or No If yes, then where?
In believers – shining his light as believers walk in the fullness of the Kingdom of God.

Ephesians 5:9 What is this parenthetical phrase talking about?
The fruit of the Spirit.
Is this verse talking about man's spirit or the <u>Holy Spirit</u>?
Is fruit contained in a fruit tree even though it looks like the tree has no fruit at the time?   <u>Yes</u> or No

Is the fruit of the Spirit contained in us even though we look like human beings? *Yes* or No

Paul lists three things that are contained in the Spirit. List them below:
1. *Goodness.*
2. *Righteousness.*
3. *Truth.*

Does that mean that a Christian who has the Spirit of God living in them already has these three fruits? *Yes* or No

Say this out loud: "In me I have goodness, righteousness and truth."

V10 When the fruit of the Spirit, listed above, is walked out in a believer's life, what does this show to others?
What is pleasing and acceptable to the Lord.

V11 Believers are not to have fellowship with what?
The unfruitful works of darkness.

The word "fellowship" is the same word for "partakers" in Revelation 18:4. In **Revelation 18:4**, what two things will happen to God's people if they partake of darkness?
1. *Partake of her sins.*
2. *Receive her plagues.*

In **Ephesians 5:11** what are believers to do with the unfruitful works of darkness?
KJV ___*Reprove*___   AOV _____
Reprove means "find fault with or demand an explanation."

V12 Fill in the blanks "For it is a (KJV)__*shame*__ (AOV)__*embarrassing*__ to even __*speak*__ of __*those*__ __*things*__ which are __*done*__ of them __*in*__ __*secret*__."

V13 How are things reproved or revealed?
By the light.

V14 Christ will give light to those who are two things. What are they?
1. *Those that sleep.*
2. *Those who are dead.*

He tells those who sleep to do what?
   Wake up.

He tells those who are dead to do what?
   Arise from the dead.

What will Christ give them?
   Light.

1 John 1:7 What is the advantage to living our lives in the Light of Jesus?
1. *Fellowship with one another.*
2. *The blood cleanses from all sin.*

Worksheet 8 Ephesians 5:15-27 Answer Key

V15 Six times in this letter Paul tells the Ephesians to "walk" or live life in certain ways. Write next to each verse below how believers are to live life:
1. **V 2:10** *Living according to the good works that God has already established for us to do.*
2. **V 4:1** *Honor the Lord through our actions.*
3. **V 4:17** *Not living life as the Gentiles based on pointless thinking.*
4. **V 5:2** *Demonstrate the actions of Christ's love for us in our treatment of others.*
5. **V 5:8** *Let our actions be as children of light since we are the light of the Lord on earth.*
6. **V 5:15** *Let our attitude always be aware that we are children of light.*

V16 Next to each portion of this verse write the equivalent from AOV:
"redeeming the time"   *Take advantage of every opportunity.*
"the days are evil"   *These are evil times.*

Have those evil times ended or do we *still live in them*?

V17 Because of what Paul says in V16, redeeming the time, what are they <u>not</u> to do?
   Be unwise or ignorant.
And what are they to do?
   Understanding what the will of the Lord is.
Look up the word "understand" in any source and give its meaning:
   The Greek definition implies a "putting two things together" like:
   Understanding the Lord's will in these evil days to take advantage of opportunities.

What is it that is to be "understood"?
   The Lord's will to take advantage of opportunities in these evil days.
Is this saying that believers should know what the Lord's will is? <u>Yes</u> or No

Give some examples of how we can know the Lord's will or where this information comes from:
From Jesus' life and actions. Being sensitive to the leading of the Holy Spirit.

V18 What word does Paul use from the KJV to show the extent of the drunkenness of the wine drinker?
Excess.
How much is an excessive amount? 1 drink or <u>more than one drink</u>.

Read Acts 2:1-4, 13-15 V4 What happened to these believers?
They were filled with the Spirit.
V13-15 What did outsiders think happened to them?
That they were drunk.

Acts 4:23-31 V31 What happened after they prayed and the house shook?
They were filled with the Holy Spirit.
Weren't they already filled with the Holy Spirit?
Yes.
What was the result from this infilling of the Holy Spirit?
They spoke the Word with boldness.
Do people who have too much wine tend to be very bold? <u>Yes</u> or No

Could Paul be showing another aspect of being filled with the Spirit to excess?
<u>Yes</u> or No   ****See Digging Deeper.*

Back to Ephesians: V19, 20, 21 Paul is telling the Ephesians and believers what it looks like in their lives to be filled with the Spirit. Circle the action words at the beginning of each verse. Write them below:
19 <u>*Speaking*</u>   **20** <u>*Giving   thanks*</u>   **21** <u>*Submitting*</u>

V19 To whom are they to speak these things?
Yourselves.
What are they to speak?
1. *Psalms.*   2. *Hymns.*   3. *Spiritual songs.*

What are they doing when they speak these?
1. *Singing.* 2. *Making melody.*
Where do these things happen?
   In their hearts.
To whom is this all directed?
   To the Lord.

V20 What is the next thing Paul tells them to do as part of being filled with the Spirit?
   Give thanks.
How often are they to do this?
   Always.
To whom do they give thanks?
   God and the Father.
In whose name do they give thanks?
   Our Lord Jesus Christ.

V21 What is the last thing Paul tells them to do as part of being filled with the Spirit?
   Submitting yourselves.
To whom are we to submit ourselves?
   To one another.
What does the phrase "in the fear of God" mean to you?
   With sincere reverence for God.   ***See Digging Deeper.*

V22 Who is this verse addressing?
   Wives.
What are they suppose to do? Battle, Oppose, <u>Submit,</u> Confront.

To whom are they submitting?
   Their own husbands.

What comparison does Paul use to show us what submission to our husbands should look like?
   In the same way that we submit to the Lord.

What do you do in your life to submit to the Lord?
   Put Him first, worship Him, honor Him in my actions.

V23 What reason does Paul give for wives to submit to their husbands?
He is the head.
What comparison does Paul use to show what that type of submission looks like?
As Christ is the head of the church.
Does Christ, as the head of the church, demand submission from the church or does the church submit to the leadership of Christ as a choice?
As a choice.

Read Colossians 3:23-24 V23 How does this verse say we are to do everything in our lives?
As to the Lord.
Colossians 3:24 Who do we ultimately serve?
Christ.
Where does the reward for our service to others come from?
Christ.
Would this also apply to wives that choose to submit to the leadership of their husbands?
Yes.
Read Titus 3:4 Is the word "saviour" or "savior" listed with a capital when talking about God as our Savior?   Yes.

Read Titus 3:6 Is the word "saviour" or "savior" listed with a capital when talking about Jesus as our Savior?   Yes.

Back to Ephesians 5:23 Does the word "saviour" in this verse begin with a capital or not? (in the KJV)
No.
Does this verse refer to the saving of the spirit, soul or body?
Body.
Read Romans 8:10 According to this verse what part of man has been saved by Christ?
Spirit.
Read Romans 8:23 What part of man is waiting to be redeemed?
Body.
From these verses, can we say that our physical bodies have not been redeemed or saved by Christ our Savior?   <u>Yes</u> or No

In your opinion, would the husband be head over the spiritual, <u>physical</u> or both in the wife's life?

Explain why you chose that answer?
The husband is the physical head over the wife because Christ is forever the spiritual head of both male and female. The husband provides for the physical provision and protection of the wife. Submission is a voluntary act on the part of the submitter. For further study see: http://www.awmi.net/bible/eph 05 23 Andrew Wommack Ministries

V24 To what is the church subject or submitted?
Christ.

What examples can you give that would show how the church submits to Christ? You can use examples from your own life and how you submit to Christ because you are part of the church.
Imitate Christ. I forgive because he forgives. I don't take offense because he doesn't take offense.

In the same way that the church submits to Christ, what practical application relates to husbands and wives?
Wives be subject to their husbands.

Is this saying that any woman has to submit to any man as her authority figure or just her own husband?
Just her own husband.

In what areas are wives to be subject, or submit, to their own husbands?
In everything.

Does this mean that if your husband asked you to do something that went against the Word, you would have to do it? Yes or <u>No</u>
Taken in context, the Word is always our final authority.

V25 What does Paul instruct husbands to do?
    Allow the wife to shop as often as they want.
    Send flowers weekly to their wife.
    Respect their wives.
    <u>Love their wives</u>.

What comparison does Paul use to show the love husbands should have for their wives?
> *As Christ loved the church.*

What was the ultimate example of Christ's love for the church?
> *He gave himself.*

> ***Remember, this lesson is for us, not for our spouses. It is not up to us to expect someone to do something just because we believe they should. Let the Holy Spirit speak to them. He knows how to say things in the right way.

V26 Fill in the blanks: "That he might __sanctify__ and __cleanse__ it with the __washing__ of __water__ by the __Word__."

Christ gave himself, out of his love for the church, for a two-fold purpose. Name each below:
1. Sanctify – Greek meaning: "Separate from profane things and dedicate to God. Purify."
2. Cleanse – Greek meaning: "To make clean; to free from defilement of sin and from faults."

Look up each word above, in any source, and write the meaning next to each.

What makes people clean?
> *Soap and water.*

What way has Christ established to sanctify and cleanse the church?
> *Washing.*

What is used as water in this washing of the church?
> *The Word of God.*

Read James 1:21-25 Explain what part of you is your soul?
> *Thinker, feeler, chooser. Mind, will, emotions.*

V22 How are we deceived?
> By hearing the Word and thinking on it.
> By doing things that look good to others.
> *By hearing the Word and not living it in our lives.*

V23-24 What analogy does James give of someone who hears the Word but doesn't live it in their lives?

Seeing your face in a glass or mirror.

What does that man forget after he looks in the mirror?

Who he really is in the natural.

V25 What does James call the Word in this verse?

Perfect law of liberty.

Look up the word "liberty" in any source and give its meaning:

Greek meaning: eleutheria "Living as we should, not as we please."

What does James say is the opposite of being a forgetful hearer?

Doer of the work.

What result does James give for the one who hears and does the Word?

Blessed in his deed or the work.

Back to Ephesians 5:26 Does the washing of the Word work to sanctify and cleanse if we don't do it?

No.

What do you or can you do in your own life to be washed with the Word? (Name at least two things)

Meditate on the Word – constantly think about it, what it would look like fulfilled in my life. Speak it over myself. It is personally mine, present and active in my life.

V27 What is the ultimate purpose Paul gives for Jesus sanctifying and cleansing the church?

To present it to himself.

What words are used to describe the church?

KJV ___*Glorious*___   AOV ___*Splendid*___

What two things does the verse say the church will <u>not</u> have because they have been cleansed?

1. *They are without spot.*
2. *They are without wrinkle.*

What two things will the church be when they use the Word to be cleansed?
1. *Holy.*
2. *Without blame.*

Christ sanctifies and cleanses the church so that he can present her to whom?
Himself.

Doing the Word – *Leader*
Ask anyone willing to share what scriptures they personalized and spoke over themselves this past week. Everyone benefits when we share our victories with each other.

Worksheet 9 Ephesians 5:59 – 6:9   Answer Key

V28 In the example Paul gives of Christ loving his own body, the church, enough to cleanse her, (**from verses 25-27**), how should husbands love their wives?

Fill in the blanks: "He that __loveth__ his __wife__ __loveth__ __himself__."

V29 What is it that no man/person ever hated?
  His own body.
He does two things with his flesh. What are they?
1. *Feeds it - Nourish.*

2. *Takes care of it - Cherish.*
Next to each above, write the description from AOV.

These two actions are an analogy of what?
  How Christ feeds and takes care of the animals.
  How bodies grow.
  How Christ feeds and takes care of the church.

V30 Why does Christ nourish and cherish the church?
  Because the church does everything lovingly.
  Because the church is in unity.
  Because the church is made up of men and women.
  Because the church are members/parts of His body.

What parts of His body does Paul mention?
  1. *Flesh.*   2. *Bones.*

V31 What does a man leave when being joined in marriage?
  His father and mother.
What is a man joined to in marriage?
  His wife.

Verse 31 is a quote from **Genesis 2:24**. What word is used there for the phrase "shall be joined unto" in the Ephesians quote?
   Cleave.
Look up the word "cleave" in any source and give its meaning:
   Greek meaning: dabaq means "to be joined together or to stay with."

What do the two become in marriage?
   One.
V32 What does Paul say that two becoming one flesh is?
   A great mystery.
This great mystery of a man and woman becoming one flesh is actually a great mystery of what?
   Christ and his relationship with the church.
Is this truth that you are a part of Christ's body, the church, a physical feeling or something you know to be true no matter how you feel?
   Something I know no matter how I feel.
How do you know that Paul is making a true statement about Christ and the church being one flesh?
   I trust the Bible to be truth. Christ spoke about believers being one with himself and God.

V33 In summary, what two principles of marriage does Paul give:
1. *Husbands love your wives.*
   ****See Digging Deeper.**
2. *Wives respect your husbands.*

Since we are only responsible for our portion of this verse, give at least two examples of what it looks like to respect or love your spouse?
1. *Place value in them by being thankful for their efforts.*

2. *Try doing one special thing for them per week.*

V6:1 Who is Paul addressing in this verse?
   Children.
What does he tell them to do?
   Be sure to ask for expensive things from your parents.
   Be as naughty as possible while growing up.
   <u>*Obey their parents in the Lord.*</u>

What reason does Paul give for their obedience?
Because it is right.
Do children usually want other reasons why they have to obey their parents?
<u>Yes</u> or No

What is a child's most asked question when told to do something?
Why.

V2 What else does Paul tell children to do?
Honor their father and mother.
Paul says this instruction is what?
The first commandment with a promise.
V3 What are the two aspects of the promise for children who honor their parents in the Lord?
1. *That it goes well with them.*

2. *That they live a long life.*

V4 To whom is this verse addressed?
Fathers.
What are they <u>not</u> to do?
Provoke their children.
What does the word "provoke" mean? (you can use any source)
Greek word: parorgizo means "to rouse to wrath, exasperate, anger."
To what point does Paul tell fathers to <u>NOT</u> provoke their children?
To the point of wrath or making them angry.

What two things does Paul tell fathers to do in bringing up children in the Lord?
KJV __*Nurture*__   AOV __*Discipline*__
KJV __*Admonition*__   AOV __*Instruction*__

How are these all to be done?
Of the Lord.

V5 To whom is this verse addressed?
Servants.
What are they instructed to do?
Be obedient to their masters.

According to what?
To the flesh.
List the two ways in which slaves are instructed to obey their masters:
KJV __With fear and trembling__ AOV __With fear and trembling__
KJV __With singleness of heart__ AOV __Sincere heart__

Ephesians 6:5 (Amplified Version taken from www.biblegateway.com)
"Servants (slaves), be obedient to those who are your physical masters, having respect for them and eager concern to please them, in singleness of motive *and* with all your heart, as [service] to Christ [Himself]."

List the five attitudes from this version, that shows how servants are to obey masters?
1. *Be obedient.*
2. *Respect them.*
3. *Have eager concern to please them.*
4. *In singleness of motive.*
5. *With all your heart.*

V6 What are the two ways in which slaves are <u>not</u> to serve their masters?
KJV __Eyeservice.__   AOV _____
KJV __As menpleasers.__   AOV _____

In what two ways are slaves to be obedient to their masters?
KJV *As servants of the Lord.*   AOV _____
KJV *Doing the will of God from the heart.* AOV _____

From whose heart, do you think, they are to do the will of God?
Their own hearts.

V7 Which description below could be used to describe how servants are to serve their owners?
Fearfully Reluctantly Cautiously Just barely Within reason *Enthusiastically.*

As if they were serving who?
The Lord.

As if they were **NOT** serving who?
Men.

Could this verse also tell us how we should be in our service to the Lord?
    <u>Yes</u> or No

If yes, what way is that?
    With the attitude of service.

Look up the word "enthusiasm" in any source and give its meaning:
    Merriam-Webster's online dictionary: "Strong excitement about something."

Could this verse also apply to all relationships in our lives?   <u>Yes</u> or No

***Part of your lesson for this week is to make a conscious effort to purposefully treat others, in words and actions, as though you were doing it unto the Lord. Write at the end of this worksheet what you did or said differently because you know you serve the Lord and not man.

V8 What does Paul assume that the Ephesians know?
    That God meets the need of every human being.
    That God automatically works in a persons life.
    <u>*That God rewards those who do what is right in the Lord.*</u>

Does it matter what position in life someone holds to receive rewards from the Lord?
    No.

Read Colossians 3:23-24.
The reward is part of what?
    Payment due us.   What we have earned.   <u>*Our inheritance.*</u>

We receive that inheritance because we serve who?
    The Lord Christ.

Ephesians 6:9 To whom is this verse addressed?
    Masters.

What are they to stop doing?
    Stop threatening.

What reason does Paul give for them stopping this?
    Because they are both slaves of the same master in heaven.

This verse tells masters to treat their slaves "in the same way." What verse combination below best describes what Paul means by this statement:
    Verses 6:1-3.
    Verses 6:3-4.   ***See Digging Deeper.*
    <u>Verses 6:5-7.</u>

Verses 5, 6 and 7 describe ways in which believers are to live in a slave/master relationship. Use AOV to describe how Paul relates each to our relationship with Christ and God. These are examples of how we are to treat others with unconditional love.

V5 *With sincere devotion to Christ.*
V6 *Carrying out God's will from the heart.*
V7 *Enthusiastically, as though we were serving the Lord.*

What does AOV use to describe "neither is there respect of persons with him" from the KJV?
    He doesn't distinguish between people on the basis of status.

What I did and said differently because I know that I serve the Lord and not man:

SPIRITUAL WARFARE ANSWER KEY

NOTES

Spiritual Warfare – Worksheet 1 - Answer key

<u>Who is Man and what did God give him.</u> **Read Psalm 8** KJV

Psalm 8:1 To whom is this Psalm talking?
   God.

V4 Who is being talked about in this verse? (pick one)
   Animals, God, <u>*Man*</u>, Plants.

What is the first portion of this question that is asked of God regarding man? (fill in)

   "What is __*man*__ that __*thou*__ art __*mindful*__ of him."

According to that portion of this question, what is God doing toward man?
   Thinking about him.

Who is the second portion of this question talking about? (pick one)
   Animals, God, Plants, <u>*The Son of man*</u>.

What is the second thing that God does regarding the son of man?
KJV _____*Visit him*_____ AOV _____

V5 What is the first thing the writer says about this man that God has created?
KJV   *Made him lower than angels.*
AOV

What is the second thing the writer says about this man that God has created?
KJV   *Crowned him with glory and honor.*
AOV

V6 What is the first thing the writer says about God's assignment of man in this verse?
KJV   *Have dominion over the works of your hands.*
AOV

What is the second thing the writer says about God's assignment of man in this verse?
KJV   *Put all things under his feet.*
AOV

What does man have dominion over?
The works of God's hands.
What is put under man's feet?
All things.
Who gave man dominion and put all things under his feet?
God.

Read Genesis 1:28 List below the things that man has dominion over?
Fish, fowl, birds, every living thing other than humans.

What happened to man at the fall?
Read Genesis 3:17-19 This is where God tells Adam the consequences for eating of the tree of the knowledge of Good and Evil.

Does this say that God took Adam's dominion away?
   Yes or <u>No</u>
There are two things that God did say would happen to Adam from V17 and V19. List them:
V17 *Because the ground is cursed, man will eat of it in sorrow or with toil.*

V19 *Man will sweat to eat from the ground and return to it at the end of his life.*

What is it that man <u>still has</u> over the works of God's hands from Psalm 8:6 even though man will have to work harder than he would have since he ate of the tree that God said "Do not eat of this tree"?
Dominion.

What does that mean to you to know that mankind still has dominion over the works of God's hands?
That I have dominion over the works of God's hands and the only way anyone can take that from me is if I let them.

Sin entered and what Jesus did.
Read Romans 5:12-19 V12 What entered the world by what Adam did?
Sin.
What came upon man because of sin?
Death.

Was death passed upon *all* men ever to be born on earth because of Adam's sin?   <u>Yes</u> or No

V18 By one man's offense or deviation from truth what came upon all men?
   Judgment.
By the righteous act of one man (Jesus) what was the result for all men?
   Free gift of righteousness.

Even though we were not physically with Adam eating the apple, were we still born into the same sin that Adam committed? <u>Yes</u> or No

V19 Even though we were not physically with Jesus in his death, burial and resurrection, are we still able to partake of what Jesus accomplished, making us righteous? <u>Yes</u> or No

Who is satan**?**
Read Ezekiel 28:12-19 This describes who satan was and what happened at his fall.
V14 What does this verse say that satan was?
   Anointed cherub.
What is a cherub?   Man, God, <u>Angel</u>, Demon.

Read Hebrews 1:13-14 V13 Who is being talked about in these verses?
   Angels.
V14 What does this verse say that angels are?
   1. Cute little cupids with bows.   2. Ghosts.   3. <u>Ministering spirits</u>.

To whom are angels to minister?
   The heirs of salvation.
At the very best that satan could have been, what would he have been doing in his relationship to man?
   Ministering to the heirs of salvation.
Does this say that satan is all powerful?   Yes or <u>No</u>

Does this say that satan is equal to God, in any way?   Yes or <u>No</u>

Does this say that satan is equal to man, in any way?   Yes or <u>No</u>

<u>Who has authority?</u>
Read Colossians 2:12-15
V12 What two things happen to us at the same time that something was happening to Jesus?
(Look for the verbs prior to each statement "with Him")
1. *Buried.* 2. *Risen.*

V14 What was blotted out on our behalf by what Jesus had done?
Handwriting of ordinances.
V15 What did Jesus spoil or disarm?
1. *Principalities.* 2. *Powers.*

What did he make of them?
An open show of them.
How did he make a public display or open show of them?
By triumphing over them.
What does it mean to triumph over something or someone?
To have victory over.
According to these verses, did Jesus totally defeat satan, principalities and powers?   <u>Yes</u> or No

According to these verses, should satan or principalities or powers be a problem for the believer?   Yes or <u>No</u>

<u>How to handle the devil.</u>
Read James 4:5-8
V5 God's desire is to connect with us through whom that lives within us?
Holy Spirit and our spirit.

V6 What is it that God gives?
Grace.
To whom does he give grace?
The humble.

V7 In order to have this relationship with God through the Spirit and receive more grace, what is the first thing this verse tells us to do?
Submit to God.

What does this verse tell us to do in relationship to the devil?
    Resist the devil.

What does this verse say will be the result when we resist the devil?
    He will flee.

Which meaning from the Merriam Webster's online dictionary for the word "resist" best describes how we resist the devil in light of Jesus' complete and total victory over the devil, as we submit ourselves to God: (pick one)
    To fight against, to try to stop or prevent.
    <u>*To remain strong against the force of, to not be affected or harmed by.*</u>
    To prevent yourself from doing something that you want to do.

Who is responsible to submit to God and resist the devil?
    The believer.

List some ways that you submit yourself to God:
    By doing what the Word says: don't take offense, forgive, give, sow seed. Walking out the great commission in my life: healing the sick, casting out devils, raising the dead, living a prosperous life.

List some ways that you resist the devil:
    By submitting to God the devil should not be a problem. I submit to God by: holding to the truth aside from how I feel and having a good understanding of the truth so I know when something is a lie. When we walk out the great commission, we are a constant presence to the enemy of his defeat.

<u>Where is the power now?</u>

Read Matthew 28:18 Who is speaking in this verse?
    Jesus.

What was given to Jesus?
    All power.

In what areas does this power work?
    Heaven and earth.

According to this verse, who has the power and authority now?
    JESUS.

Continue to the next page to recap what you have just learned.

Recap at the end of Spiritual Worksheet1:

Who still has dominion or rule over the work of God's hands now?
> *Mankind.*

Has satan been defeated?
> *Yes.*

Who made an open show of defeat of satan?
> *Jesus.*

Is satan a problem for the believer?
> *No.*

At the very best that satan could have been, what would he had been doing in his relationship to man?
> *Ministering to the heirs of salvation.*

How does the believer handle satan?
> *By submitting to God and resisting the devil. If we completely submit to God we will already be resisting the devil.*

Who has the authority according to Matthew 28:18?
> ***JESUS.***

Spiritual Warfare – Worksheet 2 – Answer Key

Review the Recap from Spiritual Warfare Worksheet 1 then continue.

<u>Covenant of Promise.</u>
Read Galatians 3:14-16
V16 Who is this verse talking about?
  Jesus and God.
  Satan and Jesus.
  <u>*Abraham and his Seed.*</u>

What was made to Abraham and his Seed?
 Promises.
Paul wants to make it clear that the promises were not made to whom?
 Seeds.
He explains that "And to seeds" would mean what?
As of plants.
As of weeds.
<u>*As of many.*</u>

V14 To whom is the <u>seed</u> that Paul says the promises of God were made?
 Jesus Christ.
Who resides in the believer?
 Jesus.
Are we correct in saying that the promises of God were made to Jesus and that Jesus has all power and authority? <u>Yes</u> or No

Would Jesus believe that His authority and power work over anything opposing God's will? <u>Yes</u> or No

Would Jesus completely trust what God has said regarding the promises working in a believer's life? <u>Yes</u> or No

<u>Where is the battle?</u>
Read 2 Corinthians 10:1-5 (included)
V1 What attitude did Paul say he was going to have because he was absent from them?
 Boldness.

V2 There is a boldness that Paul speaks about that he uses against others that think what of Paul and the Corinthians ?
>That they don't volunteer enough.
>That they walk in fear.
>*That they walk according to the flesh*.
>That they like the cookies and linger in the foyer.

Write below the description for "acting according to the flesh" from AOV.
_____
_____

What do you think "walk according to the flesh" looks like in someone's life?
>*Our flesh is moved by feelings and emotions, self-centered*
>*demands, and it's all about what I want. This is the thinking of the carnal*
>*mind and is also the mindset of satan at his fall.*

V3 How does Paul say that he and the Corinthians live?
>*According to the flesh.*

What is it that Paul says we do <u>not</u> do after the flesh? (pick one)
>Speak, Sing, Run, Jump, *War,* Play, Worship.

Can we say from these verses that the war that a believer fight's is not done on a fleshly or worldly level using weapons that are used in human combat?
>*Yes* or No

*** The weapons that a believer uses will be discussed in Spiritual Warfare Worksheet 3 & 4. For now it is beneficial that we understand that we don't war against human beings using human weapons.

V4 How does Paul describe what our weapons are <u>not</u>?
KJV _____*Carnal*_____ AOV _____

What word is used to describe the types of weapons we have?
>*Mighty.*

What do these weapons destroy?
  Strongholds.

What words are used to describe what the weapons do to strongholds?
KJV ___*Casting down*___   AOV _____

V5 What is the first thing that is destroyed by our weapons? KJV
  Imaginations.

What is done to this first thing?
KJV ___*Casting down*___   AOV _____

There are other words used to describe "imaginations"? Look up the words below in any source and give their meanings:
1. *Arguments – Discussion intended to persuade someone's views.*

2. *Theories – Opinions intended to make facts or events known.*

3. *Reasonings – Logical thinking that forms an opinion or judgment.*

Is Paul saying that strongholds are wrong thoughts that we allow to come into our minds?   *Yes* or No

What is the next thing listed that is destroyed by our weapons?
  High things that exalt themselves against the knowledge of God.

What words does AOV use for "high things"?

What do imaginations and high things try to do?
  Set itself up against the knowledge of God or the truth of the Word.
What is the last thing listed in this verse, that is destroyed by our weapons?
  Every thought.
What are we to do with every thought?
   Bring it to the pastor.
   Bring it to someone who cares.
   Bring it into captivity.

219

To what is that thought brought into captivity?
The obedience of Christ.

From these verses, is Paul saying that it is possible for us to cast down imaginations and capture thoughts that are not obedient to Christ and bring them into obedience to Christ?   <u>Yes</u> or No

If No, explain why:

If Yes, what do believers have that can capture thoughts and imaginations? (V4)   *Weapons.*

What percentage of the time do you think that Paul thought the weapons he speaks of will work against thoughts, imaginations and high things?
 25% of the time.   50% of the time.   75% of the time.   <u>All the time.</u>
The weapons that these verses are talking about work against what?
    Anyone I am having trouble with at the time.
    To fight every demon in hell.
    <u>Thoughts, imaginations and high things that are contrary to God.</u>
    **Remember that the weapons are used against the battle in our <u>minds.</u>

<u>How deep are our thoughts?</u>
1 Chronicles 28:9
What two things does David tell Solomon to serve God with?
1. *Loyal heart.*
2. *Willing mind.*

What two things does David say about what the Lord does in regard to the heart and mind?
1. *Searches the heart.*
2. *Understand the intents (motives) of the thoughts.*

If you seek God, will you be able to find or have a relationship with him?
    <u>Yes</u> or No

Does God know what is going on in your heart and mind?
    Yes or No

What would a willing mind that serves God be thinking?
    All the things that God has done through Jesus Christ.

Genesis 6:5
What was in man just prior to the flood?
    Wickedness.

What was the level of this wickedness? (pick one) Small, medium or *great*.

Complete this portion of **verse 5** from the KJV or NKJV:
"and that __every__ __intent__ of the __thoughts__ of his __heart__ were __only__ __evil__ __continually__."

Where were these imaginations in these people?
    In their heart.
What was the content of these imaginations?
    Evil.
How often were these evil imaginations in the thoughts of the heart of these people?
    Continually.
Can we say from this verse that thoughts don't just stay in our minds but go down to the deepest part of us, our heart?   *Yes* or No

Proverbs 4:23 What is it that comes out of the heart?
    The issues of life or everything that flows from us that we live out in our lives.

<u>What is the fight?</u>
Read Romans 8:5-8 (included)
V5 What does this verse say that those who live according to the flesh do?
KJV   *Set their minds on the things of the flesh.*
AOV _____

V6 What other phrase is used here that was the word *flesh* in verse 5?
    Carnally minded.

What happens to those who are carnally minded?
Death.
Are carnally minded people dropping like flies all around us?   Yes or <u>No</u>

If no, then does this verse mean a different kind of death than leaving this earth?   <u>Yes</u> or No

Which one of the following would best describe the death carnally minded people experience:
   The permanent end of life.
   <u>*Not being able to enjoy the benefits of a life lived with a loving Father.*</u>

What is the opposite of being carnally minded?
   Spiritually minded.
What are the results for those who choose to live their lives by the leading of the Holy Spirit?
   Life and Peace.

7 What two reasons does Paul give for the carnal mind leading to death? KJV
   Enmity against God.
   Not subject to the law God.

Write these same answers from AOV.

V8 What kind of a relationship do fleshly/carnal/self-centered people have with God?
   Cannot please God.
What is it that causes people to live without life and peace? (v6)
   Living ruled by their fleshly mind and desires.
What would you think would be examples of living fleshly minded?
   Letting feelings and emotions drive life decisions.

1 Timothy 6:12
What type of a fight does Paul tell Timothy to fight?
   Good fight of faith.

What do you think faith is?
Faith is when I am steadfast or unable to be moved from my trust in what God has said and done. I am trusting God to be who he says he is from His Word.

What do you have to fight for in a fight of faith?
When my mind begins to think in opposition to God's truth. That means I have to know what the truth is in order to know when my thoughts don't line up with His Word. Eample: God's Word says that all things are possible with God. I put limits on what God can do by determining what the results will be instead of allowing His Word to determine the results.

From this Worksheet, what have you learned about where the believer's battle is fought?
In the mind, thoughts and imaginations ruled by feelings, emotions and worldly ways.

What are two areas of thought in your own life that needs to be brought to the obedience of Christ?
1.

2.

**These are personal and do not have to be shared unless someone is comfortable sharing.

One of the weapons that we will be learning about is the Sword of the Spirit which is the Word of God. Take some time to look up a verse or verses that would cast down or take captive these wrong thoughts. List them below and personalize them and proclaim them everyday.
1.

2.

Recap Spiritual Warfare Worksheet 2

To whom was the covenant of promise made?
    Man,   Woman,   Angels,   *Jesus*.

What do our weapons pull down or overthrow and destroy?
    Strongholds.

What are these strongholds?
    Thoughts and imaginations.

What did Paul tell Timothy to fight?
    The good fight of faith.

What would our faith be in that strongholds would be trying to hold strong?
    God's truths from His Word.

Spiritual Warfare – Worksheet 3   Answer Key

Review the Recap from Spiritual Warfare Worksheet 2 then continue.

Read Ephesians 6:10-11
V10 What is the first word Paul uses to begin this section of his letter?
   Finally.   ****See Digging Deeper.*
To whom is this addressed?
   Brethren or Believers.
What two things does Paul tell these believers?
1. *Be strong in the Lord.*
2. *And in the power of His might.*

Is the believer told to be strong in his own might? Yes or <u>No</u>
If not, then whose?
   Jesus.
From the last question on Spiritual Warfare Worksheet 1, who has the power and authority now?
   Jesus.

V11 Whose armor is Paul talking about in this verse? <u>God</u> or Man
What are we to do with God's armor?
   Put on.
What will God's armor help us to do?
   Stand against the wiles of the devil.
What does AOV use for the word "wiles"?
   Greek: Cunning arts, deceit, craft, trickery.
According to **Colossians 2:12-15** Is satan a defeated foe? <u>Yes</u> or No

Read 2 Corinthians 4:4
What does satan do to get people to be tricked into walking in unbelief?
   Blinds their minds.
He would be blinding their eyes to what to get them to walk in unbelief?
   The light of the gospel.

Ephesians 6:12 What is it that we do not wrestle against?
   Flesh and blood.

Who would be "flesh and blood"?
People.

Paul says our fight is against what four entities?
1. *Principalities.*
2. *Powers.*   *****See Digging Deeper.**
3. *Rulers of the darkness of this world.*
4. *Spiritual wickedness in high places.*

From Spiritual Warfare Worksheet 2 where did we conclude that the battle was fought? On the earth, In the heavenlies, At your house, <u>In the mind</u>.

V13 What statement from **V11** is the same as what we are told to "*take unto you*" in this verse?
Whole armor of God.
What does Paul want us to be able to do while we have on the armor?
Stand.

Read Ephesians 5:16 In what kind of days were the Ephesians living?
Evil.
Have those days ended? Yes or <u>No</u>   If yes, tell me when?

Ephesians 6:13 Paul is telling us to stand after doing what?
Having done all.
In your opinion, what do you think the statement "having done all" means?
After we have used every piece of the armor, we are to be unmovable.
 *** *See Digging Deeper.*

V14 What are the first two words at the beginning of this verse.
Stand therefore.
Look up the word "stand" in any source and find the meaning that would apply here?
Greek meaning: Someone who does not hesitate but keeps his place.

What is worn as a belt or on our loins?
Truth.

John 1:14-17
What was the Word made so that the Word could dwell among us?
Flesh.
That Word was full of what two things?
   1. *Grace.*   2. *Truth.*

According to **verse 17** grace and truth are in whom?
Jesus Christ.

John 8:31-32
V32 What is it that this verse says we will know?
Truth.
Knowing that truth will do what?
Make you free.

According to **verse 31** how do we get the knowledge of this truth?
Continuing in the Word.
Write below two things you do in your own life to continue in the Word.
1. *Meditate on it. Speak it to God. Picture myself living it.*
2. *Live it.*

Is there a difference between just knowing of the Word and having an experienced knowledge of the Word?   <u>Yes</u> or No

Which one of the above types of knowing do you think will stand in the evil days?
Experienced knowing.
In your opinion, what does "experienced knowledge" of the Word look like in your own life?
Having a intimate relationship with God through the truth of the Word. Having the knowledge to counter wrong thoughts with the truth of the Word because of that relationship.

In Ephesians 6:14 What type of a breastplate is a part of the armor?
Righteousness.

2 Corinthians 5:21 Who was made sin?
Jesus.

Who was it that made Jesus sin? (v20 might help)
God.
Jesus was made sin for whom?
Believers. Only those who receive it can take part in what Jesus has done.
Did Jesus ever experience sin? <u>Yes</u> or No
Explain your answer: *Not of his own disobedience but he became sin.*

Who is the "we" in this verse?
Believers.
What were the "we" made?
Righteousness.
Who is the "him" in this verse?
Jesus.
What was the purpose in Jesus being made sin?
So that we could be made righteous.
What part do you play in being made righteous?
Believing in what God did through Jesus and receiving the benefits of what he did.
With righteousness as a part of the armor, do you <u>already possess it</u> or need to get it?
How do you or did you get righteousness?
Just receive.

Ephesians 4:21-24
v22 What are we to do with that old man?
Put him off.
Paul says that our old man was our former way of life. Even though I might have considered myself a good person before I made Jesus my Lord and Savior, what type of a worldly atmosphere was my influence?
    Where everything was perfect.
    Where nothing ever went wrong and everyone loved me.
    <u>A sinful atmosphere where satan worked to corrupt mankind</u>.

Would my old man decisions have been made by a godly or sinful influence?
Sinful.

What two things can change the former way of life I lived that was influenced by a sinful atmosphere?
V22 *Put off my former man.*
V24 *Put on the new man.*

What are two aspects of how that new man was created?
1. *In true righteousness.*
2. *Holiness.*

Ephesians 5:8,9
V8 Would "the children of light" be part of the new man from Ephesians 4:24?
   Yes.

V9 What are the three fruits of the Spirit that the new man or children of light have?
1. *Goodness.*   2. *Righteousness.*   3. *Truth.*

2 Timothy 3:16-17
V16 What is the subject of this verse?
   God, Jesus, devil, <u>*scripture,*</u> inspiration.

Scripture is profitable for what four things?
1. *Doctrine (Greek: teaching or instruction).*
2. *Reproof (Greek: how invisible things are proved [convincing us of their reality]).*
3. *Correction (Greek: improvement of life or character).*
4. *Instruction in righteousness (Greek: correcting mistakes and controlling passions).*

V17 According to this verse, what benefit does the man of God get from scripture?
   Able to leap tall buildings in a single bound.
   <u>*It will make him complete.*</u>
   Makes man strong beyond his years.
   <u>*Thoroughly furnished unto every good work.*</u>

Why would you think believers need instruction in righteousness if the new man that we are because of Jesus in us was already made righteous?
We don't know anything about being righteous. The Word shows how to be righteous.

What have you learned about righteousness? Notate with T for true, F for false.
- F I am righteous because of what I do.
- T I was made righteous because of what Jesus Christ has done.
- T I must accept that I am righteous by faith.
- F My old man is righteous.
- T I need to put off the old man and his sin influenced ways.
- T My new man was created righteous and holy.
- T I am really the new man, not the old man, he's dead.
- T My old man cannot be changed. *(Rom 6:6 The old man died with Christ)*
- F I can become more righteous by doing the Word.
- T Scripture shows me how to live out of my spirit or my new man.
- T Scripture shows me how I was made righteous.
- T To walk out righteousness in my life, I must believe that I am righteous.

**Righteousness is being as we should be, the way that God planned from the beginning. We have been made as we should be because of Jesus.

Ephesians 6:15 What kind of shoes are on our feet?
Gospel of peace.
Is there more than one type of gospel? Yes or <u>*No*</u>

Read Romans 10:15 and Isaiah 52:7 Romans 10:15 is a quote from Isaiah 52:7.
From Romans 10:15 Complete this statement from the KJV:
How beautiful are the feet of those who...
1. *Preach the gospel of peace.*
2. *Bring glad tidings of good things!*

From Isaiah 52:7 Complete this statement from the KJV:
How beautiful upon the mountains are the feet of him that...
1. *Bringeth good tidings.*
2. *Publisheth peace.*
3. *Bringeth good tidings of good.*
4. *Publisheth salvation.*
5. *Saith unto Zion, Thy God reigneth!*

Are good news, peace, glad tidings and salvation all talking about what Jesus brought to us?
   <u>Yes</u> or No

Read 2 Corinthians 5:17-21
V17 What does this verse say we are in Christ?
   A new creature.
V18 As we live in this new man, are all things of the old man or <u>of God</u>?

How are we reconciled to God?
   By Jesus.
What ministry have we been given because we are this new man?
   Reconciliation.
What do you think "reconciliation" means?
   Restore to the original relationship. Not just forgiving.
V19 What are the three aspects of what God through Christ has done for believers?
1. *Reconciling the world to himself.*
2. *Not imputing their trespasses against them.*
3. *Committing unto believers the ministry of reconciliation.*

V20 What does Paul call himself and Timothy in this verse?
   Ambassadors.
Look up the word "ambassador" and give its meaning:
   Represents his own government while living in another country. Has knowledge of the language, culture and works for peace.
Do these verses describe someone who already has the "gospel of peace"?
   Yes.

Back to Ephesians 6:15 What word does the KJV use that would be the same as being "ready to preach" when talking about the gospel?
   Preparation
What does it mean to you to be prepared to preach the gospel of peace?
   Always being ready in season and out of season. Having knowledge of and living in the gospel of peace so that I can share it at a moments notice.
In your own words, What is the gospel of peace?
   The Good News that Jesus came to exchange my life for a life filled with a relationship with a loving Father. He came to set me free.

Recap Spiritual Warfare Worksheet 3

What is the first word that Paul uses in the beginning of his talk about the armor?

Finally.

How much of the armor are we to wear?

The <u>whole</u> armor of God.

Where is the battle that is against principalities, powers, rulers and spiritual wickedness?

Against the influences of these in the mind.

What is the first piece of armor that Paul describes as a belt?

Truth.

Where do we find the truth?

In the Word of God.

What is the second piece of armor that Paul describes as a breastplate?

Righteousness.

Do we work toward righteousness or are we made righteous by what Jesus Christ has done?

Made righteous.

What is the third piece of armor that Paul describes as shoes?

The gospel of peace.

Briefly explain what is the gospel of peace?

Jesus took everything that I was and gave me everything that he is, giving me a relationship with a loving Father. We now have peace with God.

Spiritual Warfare Worksheet 4 – Answer Key
Review the Recap from Spiritual Warfare Worksheet 3 then continue.

Ephesians 6:16 What are the first two words in this verse from the KJV?

Above all.

What is a believers shield?

Faith.

What can you do with faith?

Quench all the fiery darts of the wicked one.

What does AOV call the fiery darts?

Flaming arrows.

At what are the darts shot?

Thoughts and imaginations.

***See Digging Deeper.

Hebrews 11:1 Faith consists of two aspects. List them below:
1. *Substance of things hoped for.*
2. *Evidence of things not seen.*

Is this verse saying that faith is confidence for things that are not seen but hoped for?

<u>Yes</u> or No

Hebrews 11 is the Hall of Fame of those who lived by faith. Does the same description of faith "confidence for things that are not seen but hoped for" apply in their lives as well as ours?

<u>Yes</u> or No

In the lives of those Old Testament men and women of faith, were the things they did not see but hoped for:

Things that they had decided they wanted.

<u>*Things that God had told them they would receive.*</u>

Hebrews 8:6 What kind of a covenant did Jesus obtain for believers after his death, burial and resurrection?

Better Covenant.

What are the benefits of this better covenant?

Better Promises.

Would these better promises be things that we use faith for to reach out and receive from God?

Yes.

1 Peter 1:1 To whom is Peter talking?
   To them that have obtain like precious faith.
How did they obtain that faith?
   Through the righteousness of God and Jesus Christ.

According to this verse, is faith:
   Something you have to build up in yourself to receive things from God.
   Received because of God's righteous plan through Jesus Christ.

Philemon 6 How does our faith stay effective or active?
   By acknowledging every good thing that is in me because of Christ in me.
From what you've learned so far, name two things that are in Christ Jesus?
1. *The whole of salvation – wholeness, health, prosperity, restoration, etc.*
2. *Jesus being the Word, all the promises are in him.*

Now acknowledge by your confession that those same things are in you.
   ****See Digging Deeper.*

Ephesians 6:17 What is the piece of armor mentioned first in this verse?
   Helmet.
What needs to be covered by a helmet, that needs protecting regarding your salvation?
   1. Hair.   2. Makeup.   3. Skull.   4. *Mind.*

What does the mind do? (Pick all that apply)
   1. *It thinks and reasons and drives decisions.*
   2. *It receives information from the five senses.*
   3. *It is the doorway to the heart.*

Ephesians 1:13 What did the Ephesians hear that caused them to trust in Christ?
   The Word of Truth.

What else does Paul call the word of truth?
   The gospel of their salvation.

What did the Ephesians have to do, after they heard the truth of the gospel, to receive salvation and be sealed with the Holy Spirit?

    Think good thoughts in their minds.

    Become really holy to receive.

    Trust and believe in Christ and what he had accomplished.

In your own words, explain what you believe salvation to be?
  *** *See Digging Deeper.*

What would be the benefit of having salvation as a helmet?
  *** *See Digging Deeper.*

Ephesians 6:17 What is the next piece of armor listed in this verse?
    Sword of the Spirit.

What is the sword of the Spirit?
    The Word of God.

Isaiah 55:11-12 Is this verse talking about the words that God speaks out of his mouth?
    Yes.

Would the words God speaks be the Bible? <u>Yes</u> or No

Which of the following best describes what happens to God's Words after he speaks them?

    1. They disappear.   2. They mean nothing.   3. <u>*They return to him*</u>.

There are two ways that God's words return to him. Write them below:
1. *Accomplishing what He pleases.*
2. *Prospering where He sends it.*

V12 What are the two benefits for those who live God's Word as a lifestyle?
1. *Go out with Joy.*
2. *Be led forth with Peace.*

Hebrews 4:12
What three words are used here to describe the Word of God?
1. *Quick.*
2. *Powerful.*
3. *Sharper.*
Write next to 1 & 2 above, the words used for each from AOV of the Bible.

What weaponry does the writer of Hebrews compare to the Word of God?
  Two-edged Sword.

For the statement below, write the same statement from AOV on the line:
    "piercing even to the dividing asunder"
_____

What does this two-edged sword divide or separate?
  __soul__ from the __spirit__
  __joints__ from the __marrow__

What word does AOV use for the KJV word "discerner"?

What is the two-edged sword able to discern or judge?
  Thoughts and intents of the heart.

Psalm 89:34 If God makes a covenant with anyone will he ever break or cancel that covenant? Yes or *No*

If something is spoken out of God's mouth does he ever change what he has said? Yes or *No*

2 Corinthians 1:19-20 V19 Where would you find the promises of God?
  In Christ.

V20 There are two things that the promises of God are to the believer. What are they?
1. *Yes.*   2. *Amen.*

How many of God's promises is this verse talking about?
All.
What benefit is there for God to have all His promises to man through Christ be Yes (confirmed) and Amen (accessible)?
So that God would get the glory.
In your own life, how would this happen?
God gets glory or recognition when we live the promises in our lives. As we walk in wholeness and health, lacking nothing. Unbelievers are supposed to be jealous of us and want what we have.

Ephesians 6:18 What is the subject of this verse?   Tithe,   Grace,   <u>Prayer.</u>

How often are we to pray?
Always.
Who aids us in our prayers? Our friends, The pastor, <u>The Spirit.</u>

We are to watch with perseverance and supplication for all saints. What word does AOV use for the word "watch"?
Stay alert.

1 John 5:13-15 V13 Who is John expecting to read this letter?
Those who believe on the name of the Son of God.
What is it that believers should have in God?
Confidence.
What is our confidence to be in?
    If we ask, we know he hears.
    If we know his will, we know he hears.
    <u>If we ask according to his will, we know he hears.</u>

Who would be the perfect example of someone who fulfilled God's will?
Jesus.
V15 Because we know that he hears us when we ask according to his will, what is the result?
We have what we ask for.
Does this mean that we should expect God's Word to accomplish what it is sent to accomplish? <u>Yes</u> or No

Would Isaiah 55, Hebrews 4, Psalm 89 and 2 Corinthians 1, from the study of the Sword as the Word, be saying that we could take God's promises, apply them to our lives by believing and speaking them, then we can expect God's Word to accomplish what it is supposed to accomplish because we know he hears us? <u>Yes</u> or No

Take one area where you need to stand on a promise of God, find that promise in the Word and write it below. Ask God to fulfill his promise in your life. If we know that he hears us, then we should be thanking him in anticipation every time we think of that promise.

Back to Ephesians 6:19
V19 Paul asks the Ephesians to pray that the message he speaks will confidently make what known?
   The secret plan of the gospel.
V20 How does Paul speak of himself?
   Ambassador.
Paul wants prayer for confidence to do what?
   To say what he has to say.
V21 What two things does Paul say about Tychicus?
1. *Loved brother.*
2. *Faithful servant.*

What can Tychicus tell the Ephesians about Paul?
   His situation.
V22 What reason does Paul give for sending Tychicus?
   To reassure the Ephesians about Paul.
V23 Paul is talking about whom in this verse?
   Brothers and Sisters.
What two things does Paul want them to have?
1. *Love.*   2. *Faith.*
Who are the two people that peace and love with faith come from?
1. *God the Father.*
2. *The Lord Jesus Christ.*

V24 Write out Paul's closing statement below.
   Grace be with all them that love our Lord Jesus Christ in sincerity. Amen.

What is it that Paul desires for the Ephesians to have?
Grace.

Recap Spiritual Warfare
Who still has dominion or rule over the work of God's hands now?
Mankind.
Has satan been defeated?
Yes.
Who made an open show of defeat of satan?
Jesus.
Is satan a problem for the believer?
No.
At the very best that satan could have been, what would he had been doing in relationship to man?
Ministering to the heirs of salvation.
How does the believer handle satan?
By submitting to God and resisting the devil. If we completely submit to God we will already be resisting the devil.
To whom was the covenant of promise made?
Man, Woman, Angels, <u>Jesus</u>.
What do our weapons pull down or overthrow and destroy?
Strongholds.
What are these strongholds?
Thoughts and imaginations.
What are these thoughts and imaginations against?
Trying to steal our faith.
What would our faith be in that strongholds would be trying to hold strong?
The Word of God that works in our lives.
How much of the armor are we to wear?
The whole armor.
Where is the battle that is against principalities, powers, rulers and spiritual wickedness?
IN OUR MINDS.
Do you have your armor on all the time?
Yes.
Is there any reason to ever take it off?
NO!

Write below those things that stood out to you, changed your thinking or affected your life from the study of Ephesians. (Writing things out is another way to help your mind and heart retain information and grow.)

KNOWING JESUS

I had the great joy of being present when a wonderful friend of mine asked Jesus to be Lord and Savior of her life. It was an exciting moment for all of us. She thought she knew God her entire life but never realized what the Bible says about asking Jesus to come in and be a presence in her life. My friend's life has never been the same since.

This too can be what you have been looking for your whole life. Romans 10:9-10 says that it takes the confession of our mouth and a belief in our heart to receive the fulness of all that God has for us.

> *"That if thou shalt confess with thy mouth the Lord Jesus, and shalt believe in thine heart that God hath raised him from the dead, thou shalt be saved. For with the heart man believeth unto righteousness; and with the mouth confession is made unto salvation."*

John 3:16 says that God gave Jesus so that whoever believes in what Jesus has done will receive eternal life. According to John 17:3-4 eternal life is knowing or having an intimate relationship with God through Jesus. The only way to do this is to ask Jesus to come into your heart and be your Lord and Savior. That's how simple it is. God's desire is to have a relationship with you, His beloved creation.

Ask Jesus to come into your heart today. When you do, He will come in and be with you. You will never be alone again.

When you ask Jesus to be your Lord and Savior you become a new creation 1 Corinthians 5:17. Your spirit man is brand new. Begin reading your Bible starting with the gospel of John in the New Testament. Then read the remainder of the New Testament before reading the Old Testament to get to know Jesus and understand the wonderful relationship that has just begun in your life.

We want to help you on this journey in your new life with Christ. Contact us using the information below so that we can send you information on how to live this New Life.

God Bless You!!!

TrueJoy Publications, L.L.C.   OR   truejoypublications@gmail.com
P.O. Box 311
Rockford, Mi 49341

www.ingramcontent.com/pod-product-compliance
Lightning Source LLC
Chambersburg PA
CBHW080553090426
42735CB00016B/3218